Copyright © 2011 By Marybeth Rombach Nelson

Published in the United States by: I Know Content MB LLC

Illustrated By Natalie Jane Estep

All right reserved. No part of this book may be reproduced in any form. The intent of the author is only to offer information for self-help for emotional and spiritual well-being. The author assumes no responsibility for your actions.

ISBN#978-0-9853966-0-2

Printed in the United States of America

Thank You God For Today

Thank You God For Today

I woke up one morning and there was peace.

You too can have peace in your life.

Marybeth Rombach Nelson

I Know Content MB LLC

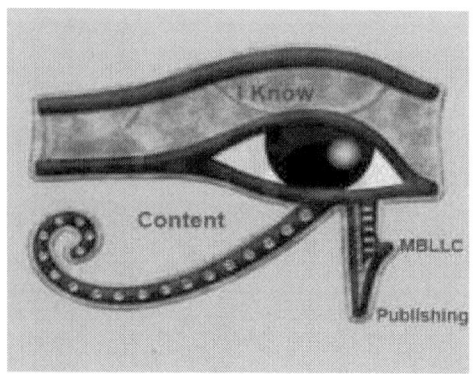

"Thank you God for today

Thank you for the quiet

Thank you for the peace

Thank you God for my life

Thank you for giving me the strength to leave

Thank you for giving me back to me"

Preface: My Healing Process from Abuse

After the abuse, I went through a process of anger, fear and finally letting go. This book unfolds through the stages I went through in healing myself. To forgive the abuser is healing to your soul. In this book the names have been changed. The story is real. I believe people with addictions, mental illness and mood disorders deserve to get professional help and live a good life. The abuser needs to get the help for themselves and to do the hard work it takes to get better. As a healed person I forgive any and all abuse. I offer it up to God.

To women in an abusive relationship,

The change needs to come from you, leave your abusive partner and find peace. I know you are stronger than you think you are, and you are not alone. There is hope for tomorrow to be a better day. My wish is through my pain, I can help other women reach out for help and healing.

Contents

Chapter 1: When it all started..1

Chapter 2: The Birth of my Twins and Third Daughter..............14

Chapter 3: Drinking, Drugs and Abuse/Leave For The Children Don't Stay for Them...27

Chapter 4: No More Pain, Regaining Courage..........................40

Chapter 5: Take Back Control of Your Life................................50

Chapter 6: Create Change in Your Life 54

"The Best Way To Predict Your Future is to Create it"
Chapter 7: Heal Yourself Let Go and Let God...........................60

Chapter 8: Love Yourself and Know Who You are Before You Move On and History Won't Repeat Itself.................................65

Chapter 9: Thank You God For Today.......................................75

Chapter 10: Resources For Help in Getting Out of a Dysfunctional Relationship..81

Heartfelt thanks go to the following people who helped me through the storm:

Pat   Janet   Judy

Robin S.   Cheryl S.   Mary Helen

Brittany   Barbara   Bridget

The Jury   Craig D.   Andy

In Loving Memory of,

Virginia & Joseph

Joe

Marsha

I made it through because of all of you!

Marybeth Rombach Nelson

Chapter 1,
When it all started

It was the summer of 1984 I had just graduated from High School the month earlier. It was a hot August night in Michigan; I was out dancing and met someone who would put my life in turmoil for the next 17 years. I was under age and in a bar; I loved to dance. I met Dick, he was older than me and had a very dysfunctional childhood. I would find this out much later. Although outwardly Dick seemed charismatic and fun. You never really know what you are getting into, when you start a relationship. Do you really know that person? Do you ever know who the real person is? Addicts are so clever and manipulative, they let you believe they are one way when they really are quite another. Be it a drug addict, sex addict or alcoholic, do we ever know the real person? I was looking for someone whom was fun and outgoing like myself. He seemed to possess all of these qualities.

Thank You God For Today
A self-help book on domestic abuse

At first we went dancing and had fun, he was always positive and encouraging in the beginning. He would compliment me constantly, "I'm so lucky to be with you" or "you are so beautiful" were some of his favorites. What girl doesn't like to hear this? Does this mod-us operand i sound familiar to you?

It didn't take very long before he would change and I would see the real person he was. I was very naive; he would cry after an explosive fight, where he had thrown things and called me vicious names and expect everything to be alright.

He constantly accused me of cheating on him. I call this the mirror effect; he was projecting on me what he was doing.

The drinking seemed fun at first, but after some time went by it got old. But he didn't stop, the mood swings became worse, he would cry and say he needed me to get better. He was so selfish and whatever made him feel good is what he did, not caring about anyone else in his life but himself. It was like he had no empathy for other people, even people who were close to him. He was apathetic in every way to me. He would figure out what I wanted to hear. He would convincingly tell me those words, while staring directly into my eyes and lying.

To give an example, if he was late after work, he would say he helped a co-worker move something at their house and forgot to call. There were always a million and one excuses. What is so scary is that I believed him. Why wouldn't I though, if you are honest yourself, you assume the other person that you are in a relationship with is too. Assumptions can get you into a big mess.

Early in the relationship, flattery and compliments were bountiful. As the relationship became more advanced, it turned into control and abuse.

Marybeth Rombach Nelson

He was obsessed with getting married and having children. I was so young and didn't realize this was his way of getting me in a position where he wanted me. Does any of this sound familiar to you?

My birth control failed because I was on antibiotics too. Back then they didn't warn you of the side effect antibiotics can have of canceling out your birth control pill. Not only was I pregnant but with twins! We ended up getting married in 1987, I know you can ask me why I got pregnant and then married him knowing his tendencies. Day to day the relationship gets to be a habit.

If you are out there and something does not feel right, it isn't! The flip from compliments to then derogatory statements didn't feel good at all. Trust your gut, if is doesn't feel right then it isn't. Listen to the inner voice, it never lies to you. My self esteem began to fall as he wore me down on a daily basis. The worst thing I did was to get married. Things only worsened, violence, drinking and fighting. He would arrive home drunk and pull me off the couch while he was hurling insults at me. Calling me stupid, fat and wanting a fight. It didn't matter that I was pregnant with twins, he really didn't care.

Dick only cared about what made him feel good. I truly believe he didn't love himself. You have to love yourself before you can love anyone else. He was miserable in his own skin and he hated people who were confident, yet he was drawn to them at the same time. Like an internal struggle going on with in him. Not the way anyone should live. Please if you are in this kind of situation get out now not later.

The day we were married, he told me "you are mine now" as he carried me over the threshold, like I was his new possession. He said this to me as we returned to our house. This made me sick to my stomach, but I felt it was too late to get out now.

Thank You God For Today
A self-help book on domestic abuse

The lesson I learned the hard way is it is never too late to get out. He would come home drunk and want to fight. I would get mad and oblige him. It was a sick dance that we kept repeating day in day out. We would scream at each other until he went and passed out. Life was a sad existence and I never knew what mood he would be in when he came home. On rare occasions he would be in a good mood and be pleasant. That is why so many women stay, because it isn't bad all of the time.

    If the bad days far out weigh the good days it is time to pack your bags and make a plan on how to get out. Life happens and you get involved in your daily work. Days become months, become years and your life is passing you by. God wants you to be happy and if you are not it is up to you to change your circumstances. No one else can do it for you. You do have the strength and courage to make the changes needed in your life. You just have to believe it! Take action to change your life. I always tried to diffuse the situation any way I could. Not talking to him when he wanted to fight and that only made him even madder.

    When I would talk to him in this state of rage, he just wanted to fight period. I couldn't win either way, I was doomed. You can not change someone else. The only one you can change is you. A favorite quote of mine is "The best way to predict your future is to create it." *Abraham Lincoln* Make a better future for you. You deserve it, do not waste your life in misery! Do not ever allow someone to have power over you. Addicts and people with Bi-polar, often self medicate themselves with marijuana or alcohol or other drugs of choice. They think this will take the edge off of their moods and really it makes their mood ten times worse! They can't stop using either, like the sex addict can't stop having dangerous sex. It is like a compulsion that is out of control.

Marybeth Rombach Nelson

There is help out there with medication and therapy, but that has to come from them. You can't do it for them, only they can get help for themselves.

They will tell you they need you to help them and that is the only way they will get better, this is a way of convincing you into staying. Or really manipulating you into staying. He would say you are the only person that can help me get better. Not at all, they have to do it for themselves, you can only change you. Don't be manipulated by them, it is only keeping them dysfunctional. The word co-dependence comes to mind, the definition for co-dependence is, loosely defined as someone who exhibits too much and often inappropriate, caring for person who depends on him or her. *Twelve-Step Program advocates Wikipedia,*

"A codependent, or obviously needy parties may have emotional, physical, financial difficulties, or addictions they seemingly are unable to surmount. The codependent party exhibits behavior which controls, makes excuses for, pities and takes other actions to perpetuate the obviously needy party's condition, because of their desire to be needed and fear of doing anything that would change the relationship. Symptoms of co-dependence are controlling behavior, distrust, perfectionism, avoidance of feeling, problems with intimacy, excessive care taking, hyper vigilance or physical illness related to stress. Co-dependence is often accompanied by clinical depression, as the codependent person succumbs to feelings of frustration or sadness over an inability to improve the situation." Wikipedia

Wow did this fit my behavior in the relationship. I pitied him, made excuses for him, was a caretaker and I am a perfectionist. Do you fit any of these descriptions. When I was twelve years old, I helped my mother Virginia care for my father Joseph who was sick and I became a natural caregiver.

Thank You God For Today
A self-help book on domestic abuse

This can be a good character trait in certain situations and not in others. Not in a romantic relationship that is supposed to consist of two people who are equal partners that love each other. It just is not healthy for you. It was a very unhealthy relationship.

There is no shame in admitting you are doing this, it is the first step to changing your behavior. Acknowledge it as a fact and take actions to change. You can only change you! A marriage should be two equal partners supporting each others goals and mutual love.

I happened upon this word in a book and was intrigued to look up the definition. When I read it the hair on my arm stood up, this is what I lived! Read the definition and see if it applies to your situation.

Svengali definition: a person with evil intent manipulates another into doing what is desired. It is frequently used for any kind of coach who seems to exercise and extreme degree of domination over a performer (especially if the person is female or believes he or she can only perform in the presence of the coach). *Wikipedia*

Referring to the previous page, the addict tells you that only you can help them, thus keeping you enthralled in their mess. I was enabling him, by feeling sorry for him and cleaning up his messes. He would be late for work or miss work all together. I would call in for him and say he was sick. What should have happened is he should have handled the situation or been fired. He was being irresponsible by not going to work and should have had a consequence for his actions.

He was looking to me to make every decision. If you are currently living in this situation, you feel more like a mother to the boyfriend, girlfriend, husband or wife.

You are being codependent, stop making excuses for them and let the chips fall where they may. I will say it again you deserve a equal partner.

The lies are so many, you can not count them, and they want you to believe they are not drinking or doing drugs or having multiple sex partners. What is the old saying "it is easy to deceive if you want to believe."

Keep a daily journal of what is happening that day and what they say, this is really a help to give you clarification. It will start to jump out to you that the words coming from their mouths do not match their actions. He was being a hypocrite; acting in a way that contradicts his supposed beliefs and actions. An example I only want to have sex with you, you are the only one; when actually they have a personal ad in the paper to meet women for extra marital sex. Another old saying is "actions speak louder than words." Keep the journal to yourself; do not share with them what you are doing. This is also important if abuse is taking place. A daily journal with dates, times and what happened can be used in court or for a Personal Protection Order if abuse is occurring.

In the beginning years, being so naive I thought I can change him and help him get better. That won't happen; you just get into a deeper and deeper mess. Like quicksand that you can't get out of! You are not alone. I think a lot of people in abusive relationships are perfectionist. You feel you can accomplish the task of helping or changing the addict, wrong! What is so bad is they tell you this repeatedly, it is so hard to see when you are in it. I know I have been there and now it is as plain as the nose on my face. Do not feel ashamed, for this happening to you. An honest person trusts and believes their partner, what is so bad about that, nothing. What is bad is realizing how miserable you are and staying. You should not be quieted into staying with this person by anyone.

Thank You God For Today
A self-help book on domestic abuse

Listen to your instincts, that inner voice that talks to you intuitively. It never steers you in the wrong direction. If only I would have listened, 17 long painful years would have been avoided. I knew on my wedding day, when he told me now your mine. A chill went right through me. Have you had a defining moment like that? It is never too late to listen and act on your inner voices message.

My inner voice was telling me to run in the other direction but my husband at the time, was so controlling over me. The thought of angering him and leaving was very scary; so I stayed and ignored my inner voice. You need to be strong and take back your life. Leave do not stay for more abuse.

Abuse

Fear of saying or doing what will set him off!

They tell you they will kill you if you leave and you believe them. But it is better to have mustered up the strength to leave and have a chance of living. They may very well kill you even if you stay, so you have nothing to lose and everything to gain by leaving. This is their way of keeping you where they want you, under their control and abuse. Choose to stop the abuse! Leave, leave, leave people are there for you to help. Do not stay for the children do not stay for the financial risk and do not stay for a place to live. Leave, leave, leave! Do you want your children to marry the same type of person and also live a life of hell? Of course not!

Children live as they have lived. Be a good example, give them peace and happiness. If only I could have realized how much damage the children experienced by living in constant fear and walking on egg shells.

Marybeth Rombach Nelson

I would have left so much sooner than I did. When you are living this way on a daily basis your adrenaline is on so much you do not even realize how very bad it is. It really hits you when you are out of the situation and you have peace in your life. I have reflected on how I could have stayed so long? Days blended together and a numbness sets in.

Do not look back, look forward and take it a day at a time. You are doing the children a grave disservice by staying. I was talking to a 62 year old woman who still relives the nightmare of her childhood, because her mother stayed with an abusive drunk, her father, who was mean and her mother would tell her he wasn't always like this. The point is it didn't change the fact that the family was living in hell on a daily basis.

My pastor once told me, God does not want you to live this way; God wants you to have peace and to be happy. That was a pivotal day for me to decide to leave; nothing could change my mind and I was ready to walk naked down the street if I had to, figuratively of course. No one or no thing could change my mind, money didn't matter, his words meant nothing now. I had decided to take my life back and leave. He no longer had power over me, <u>I took my personal power back for myself.</u>

Make a plan and get help. File a Personal Protection Order at your city court house. Read through what the rules are and educate yourself. Every single time the abuser breaks the PPO order you must write down the date, time and what happened. Then go with your PPO order to the police station and make a report. Or call if the police will come out and take a report.

The abuser who broke the rules of the PPO order will have to appear before the judge. The judge does not like it when their orders are broken! This is when it is important to have kept a journal or notebook with everything that has gone on to document everything for the court records.

Thank You God For Today
A self-help book on domestic abuse

You can point out with respect to the judge how the abuser violated the PPO order. How the abuser disregarded the judge's orders. Never assume or be over confident cross every t and dot every I. What seems like a sure win, can be thrown out if you do not have the paperwork filed correctly and written notes with pertinent information describing what has occurred. Keep track of all of the facts, phone calls, drive bys and anything that violated the conditions of the PPO order.

Keep a notebook that you specifically write down all dates, times and what happened. If a phone message was left save them. Follow through with a police report every single time a violation occurs.

In many states there are new stalking laws on the books and you can file stalking paperwork too. No one has a right to disrupt your life, take away your peace and life. I will say it again keep records write down in a daily planner or notebook, what happens times, dates, be specific and paint a picture with your words. You are choosing not to be a victim any longer! Keep voice-mails left on answering machines, take the tape out and label it for court. Or if it is a message on your cell phone voice-mail copy the message, time and date to another recorder. Label the tapes for court date time etc.

The abuser will try to manipulate the system and the court. Stay calm, state the facts, tell the court how you feel and felt at the time of the abuse. Speaking with passion is a powerful thing that can be felt with in the court room. Your heart is hurting let them feel it; do not be ashamed by the emotions that pour out of you. Of course you are hurting and it has to stop.

I was pregnant with my twins when I got married and good old Catholic guilt made me feel like I had to get married. Of course I didn't have to.

Marybeth Rombach Nelson

What a huge mistake that was, in retrospect no father is better than an abusive father! I was only 20 years old and life had not taught me the tough lessons that were in store for me. I would learn the hard way, unfortunately. I am sorry to my children that they didn't have a better father and childhood.

The pain and hell of life was almost not worth living at times, the sadness and stress of daily walking on egg shells not wanting to set him off for no apparent reason. His moods would change like the wind.

Once I bought the wrong brand of charcoal and he went berserk in the parking lot where he was waiting in the car for me. It was enough to take him over the edge and take the rest of us with him. He ranted in the parking lot you stupid bitch! How humiliating for me. The children's school teacher happened to be in the parking lot also and heard him. Can you think of similar events that you have lived through?

Think about yourself think of your children. The children will live their life from what they have experienced growing up. Either by picking a partner similar to the abuser or becoming the abusive person. Is this what you want for your children?

I looked at every day with the possibility of change being possible. It was shocking to me; I grew up in a loving home. My parents only fought twice in my life that I can remember and they never disrespected each other. Of course, I thought life was going to be similar to what my parents had. Oh how wrong I was. My husband was evil, manipulative and would say what ever it took to get his way. As our married life was starting, oh how I could see that this was not what I had bargained for.

My pride kept me from telling my family what was actually going on. They would have helped me. My abusive husband, would cry after he was abusive and beg forgiveness. Of course you want to believe so badly that it is true, but as time goes on you have it happen again and again.

Thank You God For Today
A self-help book on domestic abuse

Like a broken record, you just can not fix the scratch. Do not have foolish pride, swallow it and ask for help. Help is out there see resources in Chapter 10. When I was in college years later, I had a professor confide in me the abuse she lived through at the hands of her husband.

If you look at the statistics; this crosses all economical, social classes and races. There are many faces to domestic violence, not just one that fits. This is a world problem. Stand up and say no more! Take the power out of their words and threats, what cowards they are. They can only have power over you if you allow it. Never give away your personal power.

Pray to your higher power to give you strength to let go and get strong. Help a friend in need if they are going through this.

> My Soul
>
> My soul it weeps in sorrow over my daily existence
>
> My soul is sad and in pain
>
> My soul is barely hanging on
>
> My soul carries my burdens
>
> My soul is slowly being snuffed out
>
> My soul is squashed by my abuser

This is how I felt living under the daily hell, I was living. This is not what God wants us to feel.

Be strong and say I am not going to be a victim any longer. Take actions to change your life, go back to school, get a job if you are not working and do something toward your goal in life. Act on your plans, focus and visualize a pleasant future. Slowly you will in small ways start to feel better, even if you are not strong enough to leave yet.

Marybeth Rombach Nelson

  Create a plan for leaving and when you are strong enough leave. Look online for local resources available to you. Where there is a will there is a way! Women need to band together over *domestic violence* and put an end to accepting any form of it. Just like Mothers Against Drunk Drivers changed the laws for drunk driving. We need to change the laws for domestic abuse. Let us start a Heart-WAVE across the world. Women Against-Domestic Violence Empowerment, from my heart to yours. Let us create a wave of action in this world that will no longer tolerate domestic abuse of any kind. A Heart-WAVE to put an end to allowing abusers to continue abusing. No more abuse! Empowering women to take back their personal power and leave the abusive situation.

Thank You God For Today
A self-help book on domestic abuse

Chapter 2,
The birth of my twins and third daughter

While I was pregnant with the twins, my abuser, my husband would come home drunk and push me around. I would be watching television or reading when I would hear the gravel on the driveway and I knew he was home. My stomach would tighten up with stress. I never knew what would happen to me next. My own private hell! If I wouldn't talk to him, he would pull me off the coach and push me. Even when I was 7 months pregnant, he just didn't care if he hurt me or the babies. When the door would open at night, I never knew if it was going to be a good night or a bad one. It all depended on how drunk he was or if his mood would change at a moments notice. One night he came home stinking of stale beer and cigarettes. He was really pissed off that I didn't take the trash out. Remember I was 7 months pregnant with twins. Of course he felt justified to push me around that night. How sick this situation was.

Marybeth Rombach Nelson

This went on until I delivered the twins a t 8 months, they were 4 lb. And 5lb. And thank God they were healthy. I was so hopeful that fatherhood would change his way of thinking and living. Not a chance it only worsened. Now he was jealous of the twins and all the time it took away from him. He didn't have a good childhood and never got the attention he needed. So I always felt sorry for him, because I had such a good childhood.

My upbringing was in a loving Catholic middle class home. My parents had me late in life. You could say I was a surprise baby. I grew up with 3 older brothers, who were 18 years, 16 years and 7 years older than me. Also I have a sister 10 years older than me. I was fortunate to be surrounded by a respectful, caring and loving family. Dad worked hard to send us all to Catholic school and religion was very important to my parents. Unfortunately my father became ill when I was 12 years old. My mother took such loving care of him. I was the youngest and still at home, so I helped in his care.

My father went to Heaven when I was 14 years old. I missed his gentle nature and good humor. My mother chose not to date, she said no one could compare to your dad. My parents had a devoted marriage. I took care of my mom after her strokes and heart attack. Mom turly loved every minute of life. I can vividly remember coming home to her cooking and listening to Irish music. She loved a good time. I can recall her reciting poetry, casey at the bat with such enthusiasm. Mom went to Heaven when I was 30 years old. I wanted a relationship like my parents had.

Although it seemed I was choosing the needy mate, the guy who needed to be taken care of. A mate that had unresolved family issues and was not a whole person. This was not a good thing for me. It was a pattern I needed to break.

Thank You God For Today
A self-help book on domestic abuse

This is a big red flag, do not feel sorry for someone instead of feeling love. Growing up in an abusive family like he did, gave him the example to be abusive himself.

I was really naive to this kind of dysfunctional cycle, because I was so very lucky to have had wonderful parents. My husband had borrowed money from his mother, he told her he wanted to buy me something for giving birth to the twins. She later asked me what he bought me one day when she was visiting me in the hospital. I was surprised because he hadn't bought me anything. He had gone out and gotten drunk with the money while I was in the hospital recovering from the birth. Do you have a similar story?

You deserve so much more and so do I! He came home one night at midnight really, really drunk. He started swinging at me and I was holding one of my 8 weeks old twin baby. He went to smack me and instead smacked her in her tiny ear with his hand. This sickened me and I called my sister to help me take the baby to the Emergency room She came over and helped me take the babies to the ER. When I told the nurse what happened, I heard myself saying, "I have to leave him, because now he was hitting the baby." She just looked at me in disbelief, and said "so it is okay when he hits you?" Wow that hit home with me, what the hell had happened to me? Was I so used to being abused at this time that I took it for granted. Does this story hit a chord with you? There is no excuse for someone to hit you, leave the first time and it will end the abuse.

After this incident, I moved back with my mom for about 2 months. The baby seemed okay, from what the doctors could tell. At my mother's house, she helped me and loved me and the babies. My mother Virginia had absolutely no idea what was going on other than we were having marital problems.

Marybeth Rombach Nelson

At this time there were no divorces in our family. I grew up Catholic and attended Catholic school. Marriage was forever. Of course my husband would call me, cry and beg forgiveness.

He went to Alcoholics Anonymous for 2 months straight every day and had not drunk. This is a great program. It works for many people and I say that is great for them. It is a difficult disease to overcome.

The thing I did next was the stupidest thing I could ever do, I moved back in with him believing in him. I thought it was possible that he had quit drinking and was better. Other people have overcome this disease. People do quit drinking right? Sound like something you have talked yourself into to? What a mistake, it took about 2 weeks for him to start having severe mood swings again. Yelling over any little thing, a dry drunken mood, not a pleasant person to be around and very mean too. I wish I would have called my mom Virginia to move back in with her or figured out something else to do. But once again I let pride stop me from having peace in my life.

It is much better to ask for help when you need it, you are actually being stronger than doing nothing. When you do the same thing over and over nothing will ever change! Obvious right, but talk to people in this abusive relationship and they will share the same stories.

Anyone who has even one baby can tell you how exhausting daily life can be caring for them. I would take care of the twins mostly by myself 24/7. My sister Janet would come over, also my mother to help me sometimes. He could not help obviously, because he wouldn't and I couldn't trust him. The new drug of choice was marijuana; he already smoked like a chimney, about 2 packs a day and drank about 8 liters of caffeinated Pepsi daily. He was always on edge even without alcohol.

I have heard from so many other people that their partner stops using one drug and then substitutes another in its place, truly solving nothing.

Well that is where I was at with him and he was such a hypocrite accepting congratulations on staying sober at AA meetings. Well they didn't know the whole story, but who ever really does? I'm going to say it again the only person you can change is yourself! No matter how hard you want it to be different.

Days turned into weeks, months and years. Life is so busy and raising the twins took all of my energy. So did dealing with his mood swings. He wanted us to move out to the country, by this time the twins were 1 ½ years old and I was pregnant with a third child, so we needed a bigger house. The children were my whole heart and I love them so much.

So within 2 months we moved out to the country, which was about a half an hour away from my mom and sister. The house was an old farm house with wood floors, crystal door knobs and plenty of room. The outside had a wrap around porch, a big back yard with a huge garden and a weeping willow tree that reminded me of the one in my front yard growing up.

Once again I was optimistic that the move to the country farm house would change things, always hoping. The old saying, oh how easy it is to deceive when I want to believe. I worked on painting the kitchen and put up a country border in the kitchen to make it mine. Actually I painted every room in this house before my third child was born. The house was just far enough away from my mother and sister; that I didn't go and visit them as often. Being pregnant and having to bundle two toddlers up in the cold Michigan winter weather to go away was a challenge.

It wasn't long before he started coming home late with alcohol on his breathe and going to the golf club for hours. I was home pregnant taking care of two toddlers to chase after and I was exhausted. Strange how, I kept thinking it would be easier to stay that he would help, it was just the opposite.

It would have been so much easier without him! The children needed peace and quiet. Not fighting and drama in their life. Look at yourself why do you stay and what attracted you to this person in the first place? To make progress with yourself you need to examine your bad choice in a partner. You do not want to repeat it in your next relationship. Reflect on your current situation and learn to make better choices. Stop being the victim and create the change for yourself. Believe you deserve better and change the way you behave.

I had begun a daycare since I was home everyday with the twins and was now pregnant with my third child. This diverted me from examining my horrible marriage. It kept me busy with three additional children to care for. I had a full house. It gave me some of my own money too and adult conversation with the parents. My third child was born and the twins were not too happy about another baby coming into the house. One day they brought me her snowsuit and told me "baby go back" how cute and funny. Thank God for my children.

There were more bad days than good days. I was so busy with my children and the daycare children that days blended together. Taking care of children was a full time job and exhausting too. If you are so busy that you can't feel anything, it is not a good way to be. This is not good for you; you may be trying to avoid the painful truth of a situation. Are you making yourself so busy that you don't have time to evaluate how and what you are feeling?

Thank You God For Today
A self-help book on domestic abuse

The twins were getting older and my third child was walking now. This gave me more time to think about what was not right in my life. My husband Dick was still getting drunk or high and coming home wanting a fight. What a empty life with no true joy other than my children. What was I teaching the children by staying? We all deserved so much more out of life. Nothing in my life had changed.

What is the saying if you are doing the same thing over and over do not expect different results. Well I was getting more of the same and it should not have been a surprise.

If I cried at night in my sleep my husband would tell me to shut the f...k up and be quiet. Lovely man, what an abusive bastard! Looking back how could I have stayed? Just because I had 3 toddlers in two years was no excuse! I now realize that not leaving not only scarred the children but was teaching them negative patterns they would repeat.

The only person you can change is you. If only I would have focused on myself and the children instead of him! Things would have been so much clearer in my head. If you are always worried about the abuser, their moods, temper tantrums and reacting according to them you loose your focus on everything else. Not because you are dumb, but because is so very stressful to live this way.

The children were still fairly happy; my husband was gone most of the time. This was really a blessing, when he was gone we would laugh and read together. There was no stress, just normal peace. They slept better during the day and were more relaxed. Well so was I. When your partner comes home do you stop smiling and feel tense? If you answered yes, examine your life, why are you living like this? This is what I pondered.

Marybeth Rombach Nelson

My husband would come home and look for something to yell about. This was so stressful, I could never win! There is always something to complain about and demean me for. He would look for something to cut me down to size. He only paid attention to the children when he felt like it, how convenient to be a parent when you felt like it.

I noticed that one of the twin's language skills were not coming along as it should. Although the pediatrician was not as concerned, the twins would gibber back and forth to each other almost in another language.

The twins were old enough to attend 3 year old pre school and the teacher also noticed that the one twin was not speaking clearly. She could not be understood by the other children in class.

I had her hearing tested and her hearing in one ear was only 20 percent. The other ear was fine. This made my heart sick! I thought back to when the twins were only eight weeks old and my husband had struck the baby in the head, meaning to hit me. He had damaged her for life! This is truly disgusting; the excuse of being drunk or high is absolutely no excuse for this. I didn't say anything to the hearing Dr. about the cause. But I knew in my heart what had happened to her.

The children do not deserve to live with an addict ever, neither do you. Life is so very short and precious. If you are living in a abusive life, do not waste another day in the depths of hell with an abusive spouse! I called it walking on egg shells, be careful not to set him off! He would particularly pick on the one twin with the hearing loss. No matter what she did it was never good enough for him. This is so disturbing looking back at how he treated her. I would always defend her but the damage was done.

When we went on vacations it would be hell. It was his way or the highway! Whatever he wanted to do was the agenda for the day. If one of the kids would act up , you would think the world was going to end. In his mind the only person who could have emotions was him and only him. The twin with the hearing loss could complain a little and he would go off on this poor six year old child. I would always defend her and comfort her, but the damage was already done; she hurt so deeply trying to get her fathers approval. The other two children were more subdued and didn't fly above the radar so to speak.

They had also learned to walk on eggshells not to set him off. What had I taught them by staying in a abusive relationship? What are you teaching your children by staying in the abuse?

I remember being in the Upper Peninsula of Michigan hiking; the twin with the hearing loss also had asthma and she was having a hard time. My husband blew up at her until she was sobbing and could hardly breathe. No human being has the right to treat another person this way especially a child. I remember holding her and comforting her until her sobs subsided. Her big brown eyes were puffy and red from crying so hard, my heart just broke for her. I love my children so much.

Trying to make it work with a abusive bastard like this is clearly stupid. They will never change, the sorrow I had felt for him when I first met him because of his rotten childhood was gone. Now only hatred was the feeling in my heart, and disgust. My husband was repeating his childhood by acting out as the abuser instead of the abused child. This is a sick cycle of behavior that needs to be broken in our society. The only way is to stop it is to break the silence is to stand up and say no more. Leave the situation and get help for yourself and the children. Protect your children, they can not protect themselves.

Do not expose them on a daily basis to this kind of abuse.

On another occasion that comes to mind with the same child, she would not eat her breakfast one morning before school and he completely flipped out on her. He spanked her and left a red hand print on her butt. She was so upset that she vomited. When I got her dressed for school, I reported it to the school principal. In retrospect I should have turned him into child protective services.

At the back of this book in Chapter 10 there is a list of resources for you to utilize. I wish back when my children and I were going through this that I would have had some resources to help me step out of my living hell that I was in.

Let me help you out of yours. Personal Protection Orders are there to help you keep the abuser away from yourself and your children. Report abuse every single time it occurs. Abuse to yourself and to your children should not be tolerated at all. Zero tolerance of abuse will make it stop. Do not dance the dance with the abuser anymore. Stop yelling back; do not let their words have power over you. Someone can only have power over you if you let them. Once you get out of the situation this becomes so much clearer to you. The children were always embarrassed by my husband's moods as they got older and realized how other people behaved. Children are smart and they saw how my family acted, my brother, sister and mother. They never yelled at them like a maniac.

Also the children were going to their friends house and saw different families interacting normally. You may ask yourself why I stayed so long? I have asked myself that same question. Fear of being killed when I did leave. I felt the shame of being Catholic and of being the first divorce in my family and what they would think of me as a person and a Catholic. Fear of the children not having a father and resenting me for it.

Thank You God For Today
A self-help book on domestic abuse

My mother had become ill. I took care of her and we ended up moving in with her so I could take care of her day and night. She couldn't get out of bed by herself and she had suffered several strokes. My loving Irish mom was sadly becoming day by day more decrepit. It was a very sad time for me. I have such great love for my parents. They were kind people who taught us to do something right the first time. An important message was instilled in, me that it is nice to be important but it is more important to be nice. Words to live by treat every person with respect and dignity.

I remember days of playing the Irish Rovers, Danny boy and Galway bay records for her. To this day when I hear Danny boy it brings tears to my eyes. Mom was such a good mom and now it was like I was her mother caring for her.

It didn't make sense to me that I would end up with an asshole like my abusive husband. What I have come to realize is that he saw the caretaker in me and how I was brought up to be kind to people. My life has been so negatively affected by my abusive husband. I feel a empty soulful wound is within me. A feeling comes over me of deep and longing sadness that immobilizes me from doing anything with a clear head. I find myself asking why dear God? Why did I ever meet him? I wish I would have never laid eyes on him in my entire life! Such an evil spirited person without any kind of remorse for the pain he dispels on anyone in his path. The only good that came from him was my children. I love my children with all my heart.

He was working for a construction company and smoking pot constantly. He would work late, it was really a blessing not having him around. I was tired from taking care of my mother and 3 small children. My mom also had insomnia and would wake up at odd hours of the night.

Marybeth Rombach Nelson

Of course I still had three small children to care for too. My days were blurring into one another. So the last thing in the entire world I needed was to have to deal with his mood swings too.

He would come home late and be screaming over nothing. It was so embarrassing for me because I could not hide it any longer from my mother. Since we were living in the same house. She would get upset too, how disgusting that now my mother had to put up with this abusive son of a bitch! Exhaustion gave me no strength to deal with a divorce. It sounds so bad but I thought when my mom passes I can deal with it. A person can only bear so much pain at one time.

There were few days that were peaceful, sometimes I would take my mother around the block in her wheel chair to get her outside in the fresh air. The smells of the lilac bushes in the back yard were so refreshing to inhale and forget about all of my troubles if even for a moment. As the months went by day after day mom worsened. My back and legs were giving out lifting her constantly. I needed surgery on my legs and could not lift her anymore. It truly broke my heart to put her in a nursing home. No one else in the family could help out with her care, so I had no other choice.

Once a week I would still cook for her and visited her with the children regularly. Still exhausted I was not ready to face the dysfunction of my relationship with my husband. It was not getting any better only worse. He preferred pot and beer, the bi polar mood swings were so bad sometimes that it felt like every nerve in my body was on high alert. Never knowing when a land mind would go off. If only a moment of clarity would have come to me sooner. For it is when you step out of the situation that you see so clearly. You slow down and really think. Meditation is a great way to gain clarity.

Thank You God For Today
A self-help book on domestic abuse

Once at dinner time my husband blew up and right in front of the children said how fucking stupid I was. Yet I was the one who went to college and obtained a degree. He was keeping me down emotionally and my self esteem had really taken a hit. He loved to put everybody down; I think it made him feel better about himself. What was I showing my children by staying? My God I should have left years earlier, shame on me.

Think of all of the stars that stay too. Like the singer Whitney Houston and Bobbie Brown, Marlee Matlin and William Hurt, Rhianna and Chris Brown to mention a few. They all share stories similar of fear and abusive relationships. Even the famous and wealthy are not sheltered from this kind of domestic abuse.

Stopping the sick dance of an abusive relationship is hard. But the music has to stop or the one who is getting abused needs to stop dancing and say no more.

No body else can tell you to leave, you will do it when you are ready. When you have that moment of clarity that God speaks to your soul and you are ready to leave. When you can not stand the sight or sound of him a second longer, it is finally time to leave. You have to be ready for one hell of a storm, but after the storm is over there will be a rainbow and sunshine.

Chapter 3,
Drinking, Drugs and Abuse / Leave For The Children Don't Stay For Them

It is easy to regain who you are after you get away from the abuser. After you step away from the abusive situation it is amazing how clear your eyes will become. That fog of cut downs, belittlement and screaming that keeps you on edge is gone. I remember a feeling of peace, oh my God no one is yelling at me and belittling me every move I make. That stressful feeling in the pit of my stomach didn't hurt anymore. The silence and solitude gave me time to reflect on how pathetic my existence really was. After surgery, I had a near death experience. I remember seeing my dad whom passed away in a vision and he asked me "what are you doing with your life?" I felt such peace and calm in the moment. Love surrounded and engulfed me. It was when I was hemorrhaging after surgery and almost died in the hospital. He was calling me to action. My life was precious and I was just wasting it in a miserable, sad existence that no one should ever live.

Thank You God For Today
A self-help book on domestic abuse

This vivid thought was in my mind when I came out of emergency surgery; make your life count for something! Each and every one of us is unique and special. Life is a gift that is not to be wasted. Just the few days in the hospital gave me some distance to really look at my life and reflect on how I had been living. The scare of not having a life any longer woke me up. Along with the lasting memory of my dad's message to me. It still took me two more years to find a way out of my situation.

    I know it is crazy, but life is hard, the reality of caring for small children and earning a living alone are real. Also having the energy to go through the hell that lay before me to get out of the marriage in which my ex-husband would put me through. I knew how controlling and obsessive he was. He would make the separation and divorce as difficult as possible.

    For other separations with him had proven this, 50 calls a day at all hours of the day and night. Driving by several times a day to check on my whereabouts and stalking me when I left the house. He would try to wear me down, by this crazy behavior. My determination had to 100 percent and I knew at the end of it all I would get my life back. He would call and cry and threaten to commit suicide. He would take pills and drink all day and night and beg me to take him back. He would proclaim that I am the only person that can help him. This would also turn into I am the reason for every problem when his mood flipped. For he is an alcoholic and has bipolar disease which is a deadly combination to have, his therapist also told me that his suicidal tendencies can easily turn homicidal.

    I had gotten to the point of wanting to get out of the relationship bad enough that I was willing to risk death. For everyday I stayed in a miserable relationship with him a little more of me died. Life is way to short to waste it in constant misery and pain. Stress washed over my body on a daily basis anyway.

Marybeth Rombach Nelson

If I left there would eventually be peace one way or another. I was not afraid to die after my near death experience.

It was 2002 when I got Dick out of my house with the help of my brothers. Dick had drugs in the house and I had called the police. The police told me that even though I reported it, because they were in my house I could also be charged. I could also loose my children because of the drugs being in my home. Dick had to go now! He was bringing drugs into my home. I needed the drugs out and the person bringing them into my house out now! My brother and I told Dick to pack his things and go. Dick felt inferrior to other men, so he did leave. It was only with women he felt he could mistreat and threaten. It was in 2002 after the separation that the stalking behavior would continue until his arrest in 2005 for gun possession and breaking 2 different Personal Protection Orders. The sexual assualt occurred in 2004. Dick had been out of the house for 2 years and we had been separated.

I was willing to give it my all to protect my children and myself. Every time he would break the Personal Protection Order I would call and report it and if I needed to go down to the police station to report it I did.

I believed in my heart that eventually the harassment and stalking would be punished by the court. I created a paper trail. So all the events, abusive behavior he was bestowing upon me and the children would be documented. Creating a legal trail for the judge, police and me to have evidence in court to prove the abuse had occurred.

He was so manipulative in statements to the police, excuses why he was supposed to be at the house or in the neighborhood and they sometimes bought it. I would take my PPO paperwork out to the police, show them that the judge ordered him to stay away from the house and he was breaking the judge's orders, not mine.

This put it in perspective for the police officer that had answered the call. My PPO eventually worked and all the trips to the police station to report the violations paid off.

The case would go before the judge for him violating the PPO order and I could then talk to the judge about what had been happening. I also would point out to the judge that he had total disregard for the judge's orders because he repeatedly had broken the rules of the PPO. Judges do not take kindly to this and see through the manipulative banter of the abuser. Stay calm and state the facts, it is all there in the police reports to be entered into evidence in court. The prosecutor's office has a representative there for you too.

I was taking my life back and I was no longer the victim. I was an active participant in my life and would no longer tolerate such behavior.

I was growing stronger every day that I stood up for myself. No more excuses for my ex-husband on what a rough childhood he had and a pity party for him. He was the biggest martyr you could ever meet in his eyes. That is too bad for him! But it is no longer my problem; he needed medication and therapy not me! Too bad I did not realize that 15 years earlier that is why I am writing this book to maybe reach out to another woman that needs a hand to pull her out of this lethargy of abuse.

Start by keeping a journal of how you feel on a daily basis and if you have stress in your day. Writing it down is a great way to release your feelings and also gives you perspective. If your situation is like mine was, a pattern stands out of many bad days and rarely a good day with your boyfriend or spouse. Slowly there will come a day where you just can't stand another minute with your abuser, not another second!

Marybeth Rombach Nelson

You need to have a plan on how you are going to get out of the situation and act on it. Whether it is going back to college or getting at least a part time job so you can save money. Have somewhere to go that he would not think of, a hotel an hour away from where you live or a relative that lives some distance away.

Think about an escape plan and be smart about it. The most dangerous time is when you leave or ask for a separation and or a divorce. The abuser freaks out, and wants to get control back over you. Because this has been all about control not love. They feel better putting you down, because they feel so bad about themselves. The abuser is insecure, psychologically unsound and sometimes homicidal! Do not hesitate to call the police if you need to.

Always lock your car doors, house doors and keep curtains closed so no one can look into your home. Keep your cell phone charged at all times, especially if you do not have a land line phone. I always slept with a baseball bat under my bed, so sad that life had come down to this. Dick tried to scare me and cut the back window screen and did other things to frighten me. He stated "if I can't have you then no one could" and I took this as a threat that it was meant to be.

I took Dick to counseling before I asked him to move out, so that he would be under the care of a trained counselor. This not only gave me great tips on how to stay safe but, the counselor could see how mentally ill he was. I was duty to warn by two different counselors because they were afraid for my life and the children. It was very scary to live through, but thank God I did live! Some woman and children don't! I went to a hotel where a friend worked away from town and she comped a room for me. Every door that slammed that night I jumped just about out of my skin.

Thank You God For Today
A self-help book on domestic abuse

Even after a 2 year separation, there came a day when Dick came back into my home uninvited. He had left the home in 2002 when I asked him to leave with the help of my brothers. This day scarred me emotionally for life! I had unknowingly left the front door unlocked or one of the children did. All the kids had been dropped off at school. It was a cold winter morning in January in Michigan. I was alone in the house. At this time I had a tanning bed in the basement, it was a cold winter's day and I decided to tan to warm up. The date was January 9th of 2004 and a piece of me was about to be taken away, but I did not know it yet. If you have ever been in a tanning bed the fan runs and it is loud, so I could not hear anything else going on in the house. Dick had walked right into my house without me knowing it. Apparently he could hear the tanning bed in the basement running.

When I opened the door to the tanning room, my heart sank, my adrenaline was pumping for I could see Dick standing there with a crazed look in his eyes with his pants unzipped playing with his penis.

For a moment I stood there in shock, not expecting anyone especially him in my house! I moved to go past him, he blocked me, and just kept saying come on again and again. He wouldn't let me pass; I had on yoga pants and a t-shirt. I managed to get past him and run up the basement stairs with my heart pounding out of my chest, all sorts of thoughts were racing through my head, would he kill me? Will anyone hear him; will he go after the children? Oh my God what was I going to do! Dick followed me up the stairs into the kitchen. Where he pinned me up against the cupboard and the kitchen table. He was holding my wrists and pushing against me with his penis.

Marybeth Rombach Nelson

I kept pleading no to him, please stop, he just ignored me and tried to force my hand on his penis.

I was crying and pleading for him to stop and continued to say no! He reached down between my legs and put his finger into my vagina, he stated to me "you're wet so you don't really mean no." Again I said no stop! He ignored me, he proceeded to ejaculate all over me and he continued to hold me down with the other hand. I stood there looking down at my body, I was floating above myself and in disbelief as to what was happening. It was like my spirit came out of my body and was looking down at it. I had left my body and was watching the scene unfold.

I thought I was going to die and no one would help. After he was done he went and got a paper towel. He told me "to mop up the semen and give him a kiss." I refused and he said he would not leave unless I gave him a kiss. I wanted him to leave more than anything, so I did lean to him. He left I locked the door and sat on the couch in a state of shock for hours. I was supposed to drop off some charity donations for an auction and I couldn't move or talk.

I was numb for days and afraid of what he would do next. Dick had been out of the house since 2002 and I had taken him to a counselor to slowly ease him to the idea of a divorce, without him killing me. I separtated from Dick in 2002. After he sexually assaulted me he called that night upwards of 50 times wanting to talk to me, I would not take the call. The next day he came over to the house pounding on all of the windows as I hid in the bedroom. He later followed me to college where I made a police report to campus police. I went the next day and filed another Personal Protection Order as they are only good for one year in Michigan.

Thank You God For Today
A self-help book on domestic abuse

I also filed for divorce, which I knew was going to send him over the edge! The Sherriff served him with the PPO and the divorce papers came at the same time. The Sherriff explained to Dick he could not call me or stalk me anymore as it stated in the PPO order from the judge. He immediately called me and started swearing into the answering machine that he didn't give a fuck what the Sheriff told him.

I then took the tape out of the answering machine and called the police to report the violation. I was talking to a female police officer who was very nice, I explained to her what had been going on and she prodded if there was anything more. I started crying and told her about the sexual assault earlier in the week. A detective came out to my house and took my statement concerning the sexual assault. The officer went to arrest Dick for the PPO violation. He spent a few days in jail for the violation and got out. The criminal sexual assault case did not get filed yet, as it was his word against mine. *Please if something like this happens to you, call for help right away and go to the hospital do not change your clothes or a bath because you feel violated.*

He would drive by the house and watch me and I would continue to report the violations of the PPO. Dick would go back to jail again and again, the police had a sticky note above their phones pertaining to the danger Dick posed to me. Dick started to call his sister Trudy repeatedly and threatened suicide at least 9 times. He was in and out of rehab facilities with nothing helping the situation to get better. I continued to work, go to college and support my 4 children. While handling the stress of going through a divorce and being stalked.

Also my daughter Brooke who was 14 had started taking drugs and drinking to ease her bipolar that she inherited from her father. She also took to pushing me around, the stress was truly unbearable, and looking back now I do not know how I survived, emotionally, physically or financially during this time.

I continued to report all of the stalking and abusive behavior. They would put Dick in jail for a few days and then he would get out again. My advice is to be persistent with reporting all abuse; the day will come when all of the misdeeds of the abuser will pile up into a big fat pile that the police, judge and legal system can't ignore anymore. All of the dots are put together and a clear picture develops of who and what the abuser is. That day came for Dick, his sister Trudy obtained a PPO order with another judge and started reporting the violations that Dick did against her order. Now two different judges were hearing this erratic behavior and sentencing him.

It so happened one day that Trudy his sister and I were both at the court house for hearings on the personal protection orders violations in different courtrooms with different judges to sentence Dick. We both were in the prosecutor's office when Trudy came forward to an assistant prosecutor that Dick had confessed to sexually abusing me. This brought light to the report I had given month's earlier. I was so surprised, I didn't know about this! God put us both there on the same day, at the same time in the prosecutors office. The pieces of Dick's true criminal behavior were slowly being revealed. The assistant prosecutor took Trudy's statement. Dick went back to jail for a number of days again and then got out again.

A facilitators hearing was scheduled for the arrears of child support Dick did not pay, even though he was making thousands of dollars a week in construction.

I had to attend this hearing too. I knew this was going to set him off, which it sure did. Margaret the facilitator began the meeting and put it to him that if he did not pay the arrears' that he would be in jail by a certain date. He claimed he was not working, and then I told her of the cash jobs he did that I knew about.

Margaret called him out and he said "that doesn't count they were cash jobs" and clearly he was raising his voice! She asked him if he had been drinking. He answered that he had. Unbelievable that he would go drunk! Although not really, he had no character. Margaret made him leave her office. She told him one last time that he was going to jail if he did not pay his arrears. She was frightened for me and the children. She had me stay in her office until he was gone out of the parking lot.

Dick broke the PPO again that night and called me several times. I was at a wedding and did not hear my phone. He said he would be wearing orange, because he was not going to pay the back child support. Thank God I was not home that evening and neither were the children. Dick had left more messages that I did not get because I was at the wedding reception.

Upon arriving home that evening, his sister Trudy and her friend Marsha were sitting in the car waiting for me to arrive home. They got out of the car to tell me Dick had a gun and was looking for me! That I needed to leave immediately, *Dick truly was over the brink of insanity, obsession meets bipolar mixed with drugs and alcohol.* This is a deadly combination! Marsha said that we could stay at her house; she was a great friend through this ordeal. The police had been called, but the police could not find Dick. Trudy was truly trying to save us.

Marybeth Rombach Nelson

    The atmosphere in Marsha's kitchen that night was one of agonizing stress. The police were patrolling for him and still could not find him. Dick had made a statement a few weeks earlier to the children *"you are the reason I want to kill myself"*. He was looking at me and the children as liabilities that needed to be removed! Combine that with the facilitators meeting the day before and Dick was like a crazed animal backed into a corner and then let loose. Every noise that we heard made us jump! The tension coursing through my veins was unbearable.

    A thought came to me, that if they do not find him he will sober up, ditch the gun and it will be another night when I least expect it that I will get a gun in my face or the face of the children. *No way was that going to happen, I had, had enough!* Marsha had a car that Dick would not be familiar with. So I said to Trudy, Marsha lets take Marsha's car and see if we can find him. We can call in to the police if we see him. They looked at me like really! But I could not just sit there waiting to be killed! So we all loaded up in Marsha's car, with all of our cell phones out ready to call if we saw Dick's car. I thought of a pole barn where he was doing some work in the country. It was very dark in the middle of the night; the country street did not have any streetlights. So it was very eerie to drive down not being able to see much in front of the car. We drove a ¼ of a mile from the pole barn and we saw Dick's car parked in the dirt driveway with the gleam of the headlights!

Thank You God For Today
A self-help book on domestic abuse

We were all on edge being so close, we could easily get shot! Marsha called the police, told them where we were and where Dick was. It seemed like hours passed until the police arrived! My skin was on fire with nervous tension, my heart felt like it was pounding in my ears. After a short period of time, the police came and arrested Dick. Oh my God, he was going to jail this time for a while. I lived through it with the help of his sister Trudy, Marsha and the police officers.

The officers approached the car, handcuffed Dick and removed the gun that was now in the trunk. Dick could not see us, we were parked down the road with our lights off watching. A sense of relief washed over me all at once. What a night this had been, although I was no longer the victim! I took a stand and decided no more!

Unbelievably Dick called me from the jail the next morning and stated "you got your wish" even with a PPO order and him in jail, he still had the audacity to call me! I immediately called the jail back and had them block my phone number. Dick believed rules were for other people not him.

The prosecutor's office called me, I had to go in and discuss what was going to happen now. During the night of terror, when Dick was stalking me with a gun, his mother had called it in to the police and she had called her daughter Trudy. His mother had expressed that he was looking for me with a gun stolen from her house. This was her concern that the gun had come from her house, not that he was going to hurt me or her grandchildren! This explains a lot of where Dick came from.

The prosecutor had two cases now against Dick, the sexual assault and now the gun felony charges. My God it had taken years of reporting and following up with the authorities, but Dick's number was finally up! Never give up on reclaiming your life. Report any and all abuse to the authorities!

Many hearings took place in the course of a week, in front of several different judges for the PPO violations of Trudy, myself, the sexual assault and felony gun charges. This must have felt like hell week for Dick, everything was finally coming to light. All the manipulative stories would not work any longer. At the hearing for the felony gun charges his mother recanted her statements about Dick stealing the gun from her. She claimed he borrowed it. Even though we had her on a message recording stating he stole it. She obviously was not going to press charges against her son, his mother had no regard for her grandchildren lives or mine. Dick got more days in jail for the PPO violations from different judges in the two cases. Also he went for a prelim on the sexual assault case. He would be in jail for a while, even though he tried to get out for work duty, they did not allow it. The prosecutors office did not want to have two trials consecutively for the felony gun trial and the sexual assault.

So they advised me they would charge him with the sexual assault that was the stronger case. He would still be charged with possessing a gun while a PPO disallowed it. His mother recanting on her statements hurt the felony gun case. In retrospect, I wish I would have demanded them try him for both.

The call had gone in reporting the gun stolen and the fact that his mother left a message stating this on Trudy's phone. At the time it was all so overwhelming. The relief of Dick finally facing charges for what he had done to me, mixed in with the stress of all of the hearings in court recounting everything was truly exhausting.

Thank You God For Today
A self-help book on domestic abuse

Chapter 4,
No More Pain, Regaining Courage

At the preliminary hearing for the sexual assault, I had to relive the sexual assault and tell the judge exactly what happened to me. Just as had happened the morning in January of 2004 I left my body and was looking down at myself giving testimony of exactly what happened that horrible morning. It is a strange feeling, looking at yourself above yourself. I think it is your minds way of coping, by disassociating with the body that had the trauma. The victims rights women was in the room watching me and afterwards she asked me if I had a out of body experience. She had only seen a few victims experience this and she recognized the look in my eyes. I told her it was the third time in my life that this had happened to me. It was deemed there was enough evidence to go to trial. Regaining my courage to live through this one last time would be challenging but worth it.

The bond was set for an amount that Dick could have got his hands on the 10 percent needed. So I went to the Judge and did a reverse bond hearing to raise his bond. This had never been done before, the judge listened to why the bond should be higher and agreed to raise it. Thank God again! He was not able to post bond. Dick had been in jail since the night of terror in July of 2005. When he was picked up with the gun and he would be staying in jail until the trial in March 2006.

For the first time in years I could sleep at night and not have to worry about dying. I had peace in my life and no more pain on a daily basis. I only dreamed life could be like this again. Persistent reporting and doing the right thing with the authorities had afforded me peace for the first time in a long time. Knowing Dick would be locked up until March was such a relief. Never let anyone stop you from standing up for yourself. This is how change no matter how slowly happens. Slowly I was getting stronger and my courage was coming back to me. My soul was healing during this time of quiet. Body mind and spirit are so interconnected that I could feel my body repairing as the calm washed over me.

My life was improving and I could focus on my new job and what a normal life should be like. No more drama on a daily basis to deal with. I could focus on my children and enjoying my job. Going for a nice walk in the evening without having to look over my shoulder to see if he was following me. Not having to hear my cell phone ring 50 times a day from Dick calling to harass me.

No more worrying about a crazed man obsessed with me, driving by and shooting the children and me! Oh my God Thank you for Today! This new found peace made me realize what constant hell I had lived in, even after the separation and divorce no relief had come. Dick would not let go of his obsession of me.

Thank You God For Today
A self-help book on domestic abuse

My daily routine would include work, kids and some kind of exercise. Exercise is such a good stress reliever and so good for your body too. Even a walk or yoga and lifting weights can get the good endorphins going again. I tried to do at least 30 minutes of exercise a day and I really enjoyed it. Slowly my body got used to not being on fight or flight 24 hours a day, as it had been for the past few years of my life.

The children were affected by the abuse in different ways. If you think the children don't know what is going on. You are wrong! They do! Each child had a negative affect from the abuse, just because children are small they are human. My youngest had the least residule affects, because he couldn't remember all of the abuse. The girls had more to deal with. I'm so sorry for my children having to deal with this. One daughter did drugs and acted out. The other 2 have had to deal with stress and self-esteem issues. Today all 4 are thriving, smart, strong and caring individuals. I'm proud of my children.

Counseling is also good especially for the children sake to handle all of the past stress. It is a good way for you to let go and let God. To deal with all of the craziness that I had lived through and to realize that was no way to live. What were the red flags that Dick displayed? Saying I love you way too soon when we met, controlling behavior before we got married and alcohol abuse. These were a few of the flags I should have seen. The point is to learn from these patterns of behavior and avoid partners with them like the plague.

Through all of this I learned to love myself above anyone else and be true to myself. God loves me and wants me to be treated with respect. I had asked God to release me from any love for this abusive man and show me the way out of this relationship.God answered my prayers and guided me to peace.

Marybeth Rombach Nelson

This period of time before the trial enabled me to get strong emotionally, physically and mentally for the trial. The calm before the storm, so to speak. I knew that this was going to be a difficult time in my life, but then it would be over. So my focus had to be getting through the trial with out breaking down! This was difficult, because I knew I would have to relive all of the abuse in front of strangers and face Dick in court. This was going to be very unpleasant indeed.

March was nearing and I had to meet with the prosecutor to discuss the testimony that would be given for trial. I met with Andy, I looked him in the eye and said "my life is in your hands in the courtroom and my children need me alive" this truly spoke to him. I was dead serious, if Dick was not found guilty, he would eventually kill me. This I knew. So this would be the most stressful time of my life, with my life literally hanging in the balance. Andy reassured me that he would try his hardest to get a conviction. I felt he would do the best job he could. I needed to stay focused on the truth and nothing more or less. Trudy also had to go and talk to the prosecutor regarding her testimony. Her brother Dick and mother were not happy with her giving testimony for me. Trudy told the truth about the confession Dick had told her months earlier that I had no knowledge of until that fateful day at the PPO hearing in the prosecutors office. I trusted in God that this would all turn out for the best.

The trial date was here and there would be no more waiting for justice. I was scared to say the least. I had never taken part in a jury trial. Especially one that was so personal about myself and the sexual abuse. To have to talk about the stalking, obsession, bipolar disease, alcoholism that consumed Dick and tortured me was going to be hard. The jury looked like people who could be your neighbors.

Dick's family gave me dirty looks and his brother Larry said ignorant things under his breath to me. The guard had to tell him to stop it or he would have to leave. Trudy was of course sitting with me on my side of the courtroom. The looks Trudy's mom gave her were awful including the looks toward me. Tension was thick in the air and my nerves were jumping.

One by one witnesses were called and testimony was given. I had to sit in the hallway until it was my turn to testify. This was so nerve wracking. Finally the time came that it was my turn. I said God please give me the strength to get through this. I went in and was sworn in. Andy asked me questions to relay the horrible incident and what had led up to it. The jury seemed to listen emphatically, but you never know for sure. Dick's lawyer was arrogant just like Dick. He tried to twist my words and say I could have done things differently. Trying to displace what happened and somehow make Dick a martyr. His lawyer said I had called Dick crazy and insane and had not tried to get him help. All of this was untrue, I corrected him. I said Dick had bipolar disease and was an alcoholic. I tried several times to get him help.

This bantering went on for some 20 minutes or more, and the judge told his lawyer to stick with the questions. This was so awful! I stayed focused and told the truth about what happened. Every time his lawyer tried to twist my testimony, I righted it. Even one time sticking up for Dick in his disease of bipolar/alcoholic and stating Dick needed help. This was so true, it never should have gotten out of hand like this. Dick refused to get help and accept responsibility for his actions.

He created all of this through his actions, stalking, sexually abusing me and refusing to leave me alone. He disobeyed judges orders repeatedly over a two year period and now his time was up.

In Dick's testimony, he denied everything and said he did nothing wrong. He completely denied it all. Andy the prosecutor asked him direct questions, Dick was smug and arrogant. He could not give a alibi for the morning of the sexual assault. Dick even asked Andy what were you doing that morning? In a snide tone. The jury was observing this manipulative behavior and watching how agitated Dick was becoming. Trudy testified about how she tried to also help Dick get help for his bipolar/alcoholism and the numerous suicide attempts. She told of one night when Dick had admitted what he had done to me and that I would no longer talk to him because of it. She went on to tell of how Dick stalked me and was obsessed with me even after the divorce. She also expressed how unhappy her family was with her testifying for me.

We were done with all of the witnesses and the day was late. So the judge said we would come back in the morning. The jury deliberated for a couple of hours and came back with a verdict. This was the most intense few moments of my life, before the verdict was read! The verdict was guilty of 3rd degree sexual assault force and coercion! Dick would be going to jail. Thank you God for holding me up, I silently said to myself. The sentencing would be on my Birthday March 30, 2006. Not the Birthday present I was expecting, but one I would gladly take. My personal journey through hell on earth was finally over, what a release that was.

Thank You God For Today
A self-help book on domestic abuse

The victims rights women told me I could make an impact statement the morning of sentencing to the judge on how the crime had impacted me. If you have an opportunity to prepare one, please do. It helps you process and gets your feelings expressed to the judge fully. This is what I said on March 30, 2006:

Your Honor, words truly can't express the emotional distress that my children and I have lived through because of Dick. Being the object of his obsession was a living hell on earth for all of us not just myself, the children too. Upwards of 50 phone calls a day, disturbing the children and myself. He would be crying or angry or sometimes both in the same conversation. If I didn't answer then, he would get in his car and continually drive by our house, upsetting the children and disturbing our peace on a daily basis.

"On Friday morning, January 9th of 2004, Dick took a part of me. I said no several times. He disregarded me as a person. He sexually assaulted me. He took my dignity. He took my peace. He took my humility away from me. He took total control over me. This has been all about control. The continued emotional abuse went on and continued for the next two years. It's been unbearable to myself and to the children. To have the children have to go through this has been horrible. He has disregarded the judge's orders with two different PPO, many PPO violations. He has had total disrespect for authority continually. He continued to stalk me even with the Court's protection. He totally disregarded this. The peace every person deserves to have in life was taken from us for two long years. The children and I had none because of Dick. He sexually and emotionally assaulted me. My spirit and self are forever changed and damaged. No means no, and no other person has the right to destroy your spirit, who you are and what choices that you make in life."

Marybeth Rombach Nelson

"Please give Dick the maximum time in prison and take his choice and his life away from him as he has with myself and my children. Thank you."

This was a huge release for me to finally put it all together and express it to a judge who was going to sentence Dick for all that he had done. Although it was hard to stand up and say all that I had to say. It was a way of taking back my life and being a victim no more! My life was now mine again to live in peace! My courage was awakened and from this point forward nothing could stop me from accomplishing my goals. I felt like nothing could phase me after all the hell I have lived through. This made me realize how strong I really was. There would be no more pain. I chose to be happy, move forward and not to look back. Painful experiences can make you stronger and you can grow as a person.

All of the reporting, filing Personal Protection Orders, making police reports, following through with the court, prosecutor and police had finally paid off. Justice would be served on this sentencing day of March 30, 2006 my birthday. Dick was about to realize that rules were not just for other people, they were for him too.

The Judge before sentencing mentioned that "Dick was bipolar, didn't take his medicine, drank a lot and created really a situation where I don't blame her for being a little worried, not to mention the gun scenario."

Thank You God For Today
A self-help book on domestic abuse

To this Dick then responded "I'm not a violent person. I've never threatened her. I've never harmed her." The judge then responded But you have stalked her and....." I was sitting there thinking, no you have only sexually assaulted me, pushed me, verbally abused me and stalked me for over 2 years, that's all! Dick always was the victim in his mind and what a sick mind it is.

You can see from his statements that he still did not accept responsibility for what he's done or his past conduct, even at sentencing! He just didn't get it, still, he had that old mentality of being a martyr. The judge then proceeded to sentence Dick, then it was read, It will be the sentence of the court that your serve prison, go to prison, with credit for 215 days served. The minimum will be 20 months, the maximum is 25 years. His lawyer had to correct the judge because they had agreed on 15 years. The judge corrected himself and said "maximum of 15 years. You must register as an offender under the Michigan Sex offender Registration Act and comply with all the requirements of the Act. You must provide a completed copy of the Michigan Sex offenders Registration form to your field agent and your first in-person report following vacating your residence, any address change, address verification or change in your status with an institution of higher education. You must present your Michigan operator's or chauffeur's license, or personal identification card to the field agent at each in-person report. You must submit to Human Immunodeficiency Virus, (HIV) testing and complete counseling associated with HIV and AIDS. You must waive confidentiality and allow test results and medical information obtained for this test to be released to the Court. You must pay $60 state costs, $60 Crime Victim Rights Fund, I will recommend mental and alcohol treatment while you are in prison.

I am aware that the prison authorities for charges like this are far less kindly than they used to be, and so until it's more common than not, I'm addressing Miss Rombach, if they don't feel that they're ready to come out, they don't let them come out. Often parole is denied. And that the parole will be strenuously enforced. And so I am trying to hope that he is sincere and that he'll be amenable to the kind of treatment that hopefully will prevent further contact or danger to you, and for the protection of society."

The jury had found him guilty and parole would be denied several time in the coming years. Keeping Dick in prison. Dick even tried to appeal to the supreme court, the higher court agreed with the jury's verdict and denied Dick any appeal.

This was Dick's day of reckoning, rules were for him as he heard the judges words above being directed at him and that yes he was going to prison. My sense of relief was so overwhelming that it took me a whole week to calm down after this day. The pain can stop now and I needed to look forward to the future. First I gave myself a week to absorb the reality that I would no longer have constant stress from this person. I stood there silently thanking God.

Thank You God For Today
A self-help book on domestic abuse

Chapter 5,
Take Back Control of Your Life

After all of the craziness of the dysfunctional life ends, it is time to figure out what a normal day is like. This statement sounds crazy, but those of you who have lived in this sick environment know what I'm talking about. To get back on a even keel, live in the moment and enjoy the little things in life. Taking a walk with the children or just sitting down to watch TV in quiet. A calmness comes back into your life that just feels right.

Start to plan what your wants and desires are in life, do you want to go back to school to earn a degree. If so make a plan on how you can make this happen. There are grants that you can apply for. Contact a college and set up a appointment to find out what is available.

Or look for a job and create a knock out resume. Think about a position that would give you joy in your life. If you love what you are doing it doesn't even feel like work. How great is that feeling to realize that you are in control of your own life again, but really you were all along.

The thought of the control being relinquished to your abuser was wrong on your part, no one can take it away from you on a daily basis. You can leave the situation and it will stop. This is tough to see when you are in the thick of the mud and muck of a dysfunctional relationship but it is the hard truth.

This responsibility for my own life and the choices that I have made, make you realize that you are in control of your own destiny. Stop being the victim and become victorious over your own life! It is truly empowering and it is a mind set. A way of thinking positively and empowering your choices to better your life. Every single person walking on this planet has had a terrible event in their lives. Do not dwell in the misery of yesterday, it will only keep you down.

The words you speak to yourself need to be encouraging and positive. Tomorrow will be better than today. I will get a job offer that pays all of my bills and have money left over. Statements like these make you feel better, and it draws good things to you. Make a list of goals that you would like to achieve and list the steps you can take to reach them. Look at it this way, do not give another day to the stress of abuse. Do not relive it on a daily basis, if you continue to be the victim your life will not change.

Thank You God For Today
A self-help book on domestic abuse

Move out of this rut and do not give the abuser another day, minute or second of your life. Join a support group or go to counseling to get it out of you. Or even write it down, release it from your body, mind and soul. It is such a release not to carry it around with you anymore. It is as if our body is lighter and our soul is a little brighter. *"What lies behind us and what lies before us are small matters compared to what lies within us" Ralph Waldo Emerson*

Exercise can be a great healer of the mind and body. It is a good way to get the good endorphins running through out your body. Also it is good for your health and relieving stress. Exercise always helped me to focus on my goals and gave me time to let things go at the same time. When you are mindlessly on the treadmill and can clear your head it has a tranquil affect on your whole being.

Take up a hobby that is enjoyable to you. Painting, writing, knitting and even making crafts can be a way of releasing negative energy for good positive energy. I looked at this time after the trial to replenish every cell in my body with healthy positive activities and people.

Going to church helped me tremendously. Even if you are not religious, there are other things to give you the same feeling of peace, a walk in the woods or a bike ride through a park on beautiful morning. Think of ways to make yourself happy and then do them. I used to feel guilty about taking time for myself. Now I know it is unhealthy not to take care of yourself and enjoy life. Everyday is a precious gift that we should not waste in the past, or in the future we need to enjoy the now. Life goes by so fast, days become months and then years.

Marybeth Rombach Nelson

To be financially in charge of your life is empowering and makes you feel valued as a person. It also enables you to stand on your own two feet without relying on anyone else for your survival, or the survival of your children. Yes you can do it yourself, perseverance pays off.

No matter how bad your life was before, it can be as great as you can imagine it to be. It all starts with a positive thought to light the way out.

Being self sufficient empowers you to be in control of every aspect of your life. Sure you may have a boss to report to, but when the workday is done you can relax and enjoy the life that you have made for yourself. For you and only you are responsible for your life. Abusive people can't abuse you if you are not with them, can they? I see this so very clearly now, but it was hard when I was in the dysfunction. Fear keeps you frozen in time in an abusive relationship, be brave and the fear subsides.

Thank God I didn't let the following things in my life make me a poor me person. I was sexually abused and stalked. My dad died when I was 14 years old. My mom died when I was 30 years old. My brother died in his forties. A babysitter abused my children and I prosecuted them. I had a surgery and hemorrhaged afterwards. I had a near death experience that changed my life. I know not to fear death anymore. I still consider myself lucky in my life and I'm grateful for what I have. I had great parents and a wonderful family that gave me a good foundation. The near death experience, made me feel like everyday there after was a blessing.

Chapter 6,
Create Change in Your Life

"The best way to predict your future is to create it"
Abraham Lincoln

So if there is something that is not working in your life, change it. It is all up to you! Things do not just happen in your life to you, you are an active participant in it. The people that you surround yourself with, the job that you have chosen, the church that you attend, the activities that you do are all a choice. If something is lacking in your life, take the initiative to change it. You have the power to create the life that makes you happy. Figure out what that is and go for it. The only one holding you back is yourself. Jump in with both feet and decide what needs changing. Like Nike says "just do it".

"Be not a slave of your own past-plunge into the sublime seas dive deep and swim far, so you shall come back with self-respect with new power, with an advanced experience, that shall explain and over look the old." Ralph Waldo Emerson

I love this quote! Do not let your past hold you back, create the change in your life that will propel you into your future. Self-respect is so important to feel good about yourself. To move on to the new and better things that life has to offer. Life is so short we need to really live everyday to the fullest. Make each day stand for something positive, whether it be hugging your child, reading to them, take the time to enjoy today. We only have one time to live each moment, make the most of your moments.

Create a vision of change that you want to take root in your life. See it in your minds eye, write it down and say it to yourself everyday. Such as I see my job in marketing and it is everything I desire with a salary that allows me to pay my bills and still have some money left over. Now of course you need to follow this up with action. Look online for the position that you desire, apply for it and keep making affirmations to draw it to you.

Wishing something, having the thought is the beginning of what can be possible for you. Positive thinking helps everything in life, attitude is everything, in business, personal life, sports and as a parent. A good outlook always makes things seem better and enables you to come up with solutions easier than with a negative outlook. Surround yourself with uplifting people in your life. Stay away from naysayer's and Debbie downers.

Who you hang around with has a big effect on how you feel on a daily basis. Mother was right, be careful who you hang around with, you become your friends to a certain extent. Make sure you check yourself for positive thoughts and words. Be conscious of the way you think and speak. It will help you be more positive and stop patterns of negativity. Especially with someone whom has been in a dysfunctional, abusive relationship. It is so easy to be stuck in the negative experiences of the past.

Create a life where you are not dependent on anyone else to survive. Sure you can get help from family, to baby sit if you need to, or help a little financially. This is such a great relief to be able to provide for yourself and your family. No one has control over your life through dependency. Look for a job you love to do, it will be like not working if you enjoy what you are doing on a daily basis.

"Where there is dependence, there is instability, where there is no dependence, there is no instability, where there is no instability, there is quietude where there is quietude, there is no desire, where there is no desire, there is no coming or going, there is no birth or death, where there is no birth or death, there is neither this world or that world, nor both: that is the end of sorrow" Udana, Buddhist Scriptures

Marybeth Rombach Nelson

The word quietude stands out to me, peace and the end to all sorrow. What a great change to make in your life. Not to deal with the disruption of all the anger and dysfunction. Can you imagine how good that feels. I can because I have made the necessary choices in my life to change my circumstances for the better. The great news is you can too, decide on the life you want and take steps to go after it. Write it down and the steps you can take to achieve your dream life.

Uplift your spirits by playing some of your favorite music, exercise, stay active with friends and family. All of these things help us feel good. When you feel good, better ideas come to you and the direction of your life improves. Do yoga, meditate to clear your mind and quiet your soul. Exercise does this for me also, a concise vision can come to you and act on it for a better life.

"As human beings we all want to be happy and free from misery we have learned that the key to happiness is inner peace. The greatest obstacles to inner peace are disturbing emotions such as anger and attachment, fear and suspicion, while love, compassion and a sense of universal responsibility are the sources of peace and happiness. Tenzin Gyatso, the 14th Dalai Lama

Thank You God For Today
A self-help book on domestic abuse

Positive energy will surround you and propel you forward and not hold you back. Change who you are around, if the person makes you angry and upset all of the time do not hang with them. That is such a negative load to carry around with you. Drop the heavy load, be with people who make you smile and laugh. Life is so very short, enjoy each moment that you have. Make a journal entry every time you feel at peace. Write down what you were doing, where you were and how you felt. Keep doing this until a deep feeling of inner peace encompasses you. You deserve to be happy and God wants you to be happy. To have a great life! Do not get down in the dumps, and if you do cry let it all out.

Then move on, change is hard even if your situation is better. If you have been living with your adrenaline on everyday for 10 years like I was, it took some time for me to settle down and become on a normal level everyday. So cut yourself some slack and stick to the plan of creating the life you deserve. How do you go about changing something? First you have the desire for things to be different. Then you ask yourself what do I need to do to make things different? An action plan as I call it comes into play. Take a spiral notebook and write down what you want to change and how you think you can make it happen. Create a to do list and scratch them off one by one as you accomplish them. Before you know it you are on your way to having peace, quiet and happiness. Once you get started in the right direction, people seem to enter your life that will be part of the future you created.

Pat yourself on the back and be happy. All of the positive love for yourself and your life is coming back to you. Keep the everyday tasks and thoughts positive. Stay away from negative people who tell you that you can't change or you can't do something. Yes you can! Do not let them drag you down in the mud. Chances are they are miserable themselves and do not want you to be happy. Always check how you are feeling around your friends, are there friends who make you feel like they suck the life out of you. Stop being around them.

Continue to self reflect on how you feel and if your daily decisions are making the future you wish to be in. If not, set yourself straight and take daily steps to right yourself. I had a plan B and C when I left my abusive dysfunctional relationship. It is okay to keep tweaking your dream life until it is what you want it to be. Always trust your gut on how you are feeling, do you have a feeling of peace? That is what I had desired for so long and it evaded me, because I was not brave enough to create the changes that I needed. So be brave and allow your life to change for the better.

I remember praying in church to give me the life I wanted. But the bible tells you that God helps those whom help themselves. So don't feel sorry for yourself and stay stuck in the same old rut. Learn life lessons from the bad experiences you have lived through. Grow stronger and reflect how dam strong you are that you lived through them! That is amazing in itself, your coping skills and survival skills that are deep within your very being. You are an amazing person. Help others through to a life with out misery. Share the lessons that you have learned. Focus on your goals and keep improving them to create the best future for you. Just like the quote says *"The best way to predict the future is to create it."* Abraham Lincoln

Chapter 7,
Heal Yourself, Let Go and Let God

Acknowledge the mistakes you have made in the past. Forgive yourself for any and all mistakes. Allow yourself to enjoy each moment, have fun again. Play the music loud, dance sing be silly with your kids. Life is supposed to be fun and carefree not so serious all the time. Bring joy back into your life. Offer all of your pain and suffering up to God. Let it be released from your body and soul, right now. Stop right now and offer all of the suffering up to God as your sacrifice. Ah when I did this it made me feel like a lead weight had just been lifted off of my shoulders. Thank God for taking it away from you and allowing you to heal.

The healing will slowly happen, with the more joy you allow back into your life, choose to be happy. I know that does not sound easy, but it is simply your attitude toward life. The more positive you are about life the better it will be. No matter what your circumstances are be thankful for what you have.

Think about what you are doing right in your life and feel good about it. Let go of any thoughts of all the things you did wrong in your past, let them go they won't do you any good. Focus on a new vision to heal your body, mind and soul. Reflect on what you can do on a daily basis to love yourself and heal yourself. It can be small things, such as a positive affirmation, a walk or exercising to feel good. I say *"My life is getting better everyday that I am alive."*

Meditation is a great way to clear your mind and get your focus back. Yoga is a great way to relax and let go of your tension. Find what works for you and make sure you keep doing it until you feel better. Ask God to heal you and take away any suffering or anguish from you. Imagine all of your pain floating away from you up into the sky and disappearing from you.

Now imagine what you want your new life to be like. See it as if you are looking at a picture. What do you feel when you look at this picture. Write down how you can make this your reality. Change how you react to situations. Always have purpose and direction for your life. Have a goal in mind to achieve and strive for. If you want a better job, first thank God that you have a job and then start applying for the job you want. Take classes if you need to for the new job. Imagine yourself in that position. All these positive feelings will make you heal yourself.

Write down on a piece of paper all of the good qualities that you possess. See how awesome you are! God loves you and wants you to be happy. Let him heal you, forgive yourself and let go of all the pain.

If you need to go to a counselor and get everything off of your chest, do it. Sometimes we just need to tell another person and have them listen to you to feel better. Choose someone that makes you feel relaxed and at ease. A good counselor can help you heal and teach you coping mechanisms to heal yourself too. Let yourself cry and let stress leave your body.

Every decision you make should lead you to where you want to be in the future. Write down your goals, so you know where you are going and develop a plan as to how you are going to get there. Take that first step toward your future of happiness. Check daily that you are staying on track and have a balance in life of work, family and fun.

What is your personal mission statement? What is your souls purpose on earth? What do you want out of life? What makes you happy and excited about life? These are all great questions to ask yourself and figure out where you want to end up in life. Don't sit back and just let life happen to you, take positive control of your own destiny. Never give up your personal power again. Look at all of your options and alternatives, make the best choice for you. Only you can know what truly makes you excited about life and happy.

Give yourself time to make daily adjustments to your plan. Pat yourself on the back for every baby step you make. Once you are healed you will feel light as a feather again and ready to take on the world. The enthusiasm is with in you to do everything you desire.

A schedule helps one feel normal again. Having basic day to day scheduled activities that creates a new normal. Children especially need to have a sense of security and normalcy. Make sure to schedule in time for you to release stress, such as yoga every Tuesday at 7 pm. And stick to it. Children can have certain nights too, like game night every Friday at 7 pm. Have fun, enjoy the time you spend with the children and make sure they know how much you love them.

If you attend church, start going on a regular basis. Church can give you peace and uplift your mood. I remember sitting in church praying for God to release any love for my ex husband so I could move on sanely. God did answer my prayers. I felt so much lighter in spirit and even in my body. People noticed the difference in me. I had let go and let God. Even if you do not attend a church, ask your higher power to release you from your old patterns of doing things. Get healthy in the choices you make for yourself and your family. You will feel so much joy to be free of burden and misery!

Whatever it takes to heal you do it. Of course it needs to be legal. Some people love to run marathons and focus on training for the big day. This is a great way to get fit and do something good for your body. Exercising is good for the soul. Helping a charity in a marathon is a double bonus. When you give you receive. So many people are handicapped with diseases. We are lucky to be free of disease.

Helping others helps us to heal, so volunteer or join a charity. Or just volunteer for one to help others less fortunate. I have always enjoyed volunteering and it always lifts my mood to make someone else happy. Everyone has a struggle in their lives and you should never feel like you are alone. There are so many women going through domestic abuse and in need of healing. Once you have healed and feel better, send good intentions out for any women who is suffering from domestic violence. Do something to help, donate clothes, food and listen if you have a friend going through this. This helps you to give back to someone and grow as a person. Just think how far you have come, you are no longer a victim! Life is good and everything is coming together for you. Believe it, see it and make choices to make all of your wishes come true. Let go of all those nasty memories of the past and move forward. The lessons you have learned will stay with you for life.

Marybeth Rombach Nelson

Chapter 8,
Love Yourself and Know Who You are Before You Move On and History Won't Repeat Itself

That old saying you have to love yourself before you can love others is true. Think back to when you met your ex-abuser. What drew you to that person? What did they say and do in the beginning of the relationship? Were there red flags that you just ignored? When I looked back there were several red flags. Saying I love you, way too early in the relationship, calling and checking where I was all the time. These were things that should have stood out to me. It may seem flattering at the time, but did it feel good? I know when I went out with friends, they would comment on how many times he called me to check up on me. Does that sound familiar. Controlling behavior is never good. What ended up happening to me is that my friends did not like him and eventually did not want to hang out anymore.

So you end up going with the abuser and you don't want to be alone. But if your friends do not like your boyfriend, there is probably a good reason for this. It is easy to reflect on now, but it was not so easy at the time. Always think about how your gut feels, it will never steer you wrong. If it doesn't feel right, it is not! Do not ignore what your body is trying to tell you. Your inner voice is your soul trying to talk to you and guide you.

Create a list of everything you love about yourself. Feel good about who you are. Being in that feeling of love will draw love to you. Be the creator of your life and how you want to live your life. Make a list of everything that makes you happy. Self-reflection will make you aware of what makes you the happiest. Remove people from your life that bring you down and don't pick up the phone when they call. Keep your energy high and do not let others drain you. Think about what you want out of life, what is most important to you. Make a list of goals for your life and an action plan on how to achieve them. Is there something that you have always been drawn to but never explored? Take time to get to know you, slow down and keep a journal of really good days and what you were doing. Even the bad days, it is good to journal to avoid or minimize what or who you were interacting with and avoid them as much as possible.

Say out loud everyday positive affirmations, like I love me and I deserve to be happy. Positive words create a positive energy that makes you think positive and act positive. This will make life more enjoyable and draw good people towards you.

Love makes you feel good and glow with enthusiasm. Only you can make you happy. Do not look to other people to fill a void in you. Find out what you need and fill that void yourself. It is all up to you. Take responsibility for your happiness. In other words become whole as a person before you move on and you won't draw the abusive partner again.

Let go of any and all bad feelings from the past, leave them in the past. Focus on how happy your new life can be.

"Holding on to anger is like grasping a hot coal with the intent of throwing it at someone else; you are the one getting burned." Gautama Buddha, Founder of Buddhism

So move forward in your life. Don't stay in the negativity of blaming, finding fault and criticizing everyone. This never has made anyone happy. React in a positive way to everything you encounter, it is truly a choice. Choose to be happy for you! Attitude is so very important in life and it can change every aspect of your life. Stop making excuses for going after what you want in life. Take a chance and put fear aside, you will never know if you never try.

Thank You God For Today
A self-help book on domestic abuse

    Imagine your perfect life, what does it look like? Who are you interacting with? What job do you have? What daily activities are you doing? Write down what you visualize for your perfect life. Aim high and be happy. Say something good about yourself everyday. Realize you deserve to be happy. Love yourself enough to never let anyone disrespect you in any way. Never give up your personal power to anyone ever again. Never look outwardly to other people to make you happy, always look inward. Follow your passion, it won't lead you astray.

    Rely on yourself for everything you need, and you won't be disappointed. Reflect on your deepest thoughts and wishes. Introspection is soothing to the soul. Once you find out what makes you tick, you can truly give of yourself again in a relationship. Embrace the life you are making for yourself. Before you know it you will draw a special person with your new found confidence in yourself and love for yourself.

    The only person you can fix is you. So if you meet someone, go on a date and have the thought of fixing something about them don't even go out with them again. Focus on yourself and your aspirations. Don't try to change other people ever again.

Marybeth Rombach Nelson

Keep looking if there is something that you think needs fixing in a person that you date. There are plenty of fish in the sea. Don't go down the wrong road again. If you are not happy with the way the person is today, it is time to move on. There is a person who is just right for you waiting, with all of the traits that you desire. Sometimes when you are at peace with yourself and stop looking is when that person finds you.

Know that you are self sufficient and you do not need anyone but you. Have peace in your life and tranquility in your daily existence. Do not rush to meet someone. Time, reflection, vision and knowing who you are on the inside will allow you to love yourself first. Then you can move on to love someone else as a complete half of a relationship. Just as the new person should be whole themselves and able to offer you a complete other half. Never ever settle for less than what you deserve again. Life is too short not to be happy and only you can make the choices to create that special life.

Abuse is fear

Abuse is control

Abuse is stress

Abuse is low-self-esteem

Abuse is pain

Thank You God For Today
A self-help book on domestic abuse

> Peace is freedom
>
> Peace is self-reliance
>
> Peace is pure love
>
> Peace is Joy
>
> Peace is Knowing who you are
>
> Peace is Loving yourself

Which do you prefer? I choose Peace everyday of my life, it is up to me. I love myself completely everyday, because I am from God and no one will abuse me in any way again. I will set no limitation to the joy and happiness my life can become. The possibilities are limitless and infinite in my making. Empower yourself to reach new heights in life.

Marybeth Rombach Nelson

You are almost there, the point of regaining who you are and knowing what you want. The personal awakening that you have had will guide you to what brings joy into your life. You have realized how strong you are and all of the possibilities life has to offer you. The only limits out there are limits you place on yourself. So reach for the stars.

Look at where you have been in this journey of letting go of the past and creating your future.

Regaining Yourself   Getting Help

Getting Out
    Courage

<u>Abusive Relationship</u>
    Peace
Awakening   Coping

Last thoughts on loving yourself, change yourself if you are not happy. I'll say it again no one else can make you happy, it is up to you. Learn from your past pain and experiences, what you do not want in your life. Now examine what not to repeat. Choose to be different in your thoughts, actions and intentions. Do not perpetuate the same pattern again and again. This is so important to acknowledge that you have all the control over your life and only you.

Heal the parts of your personality that need healing. Be grateful, joyful and energetic. Do not dwell on the past and play the victim. Become empowered and never choose to be a victim again! Every choice has a consequence and only you can choose. Always pay attention to how you feel in every situation and never ever doubt yourself. Listen to your inner voice, when it talks to you. If something does not feel right it is not. Eliminate fear and live in love. Feel the anxiety lift from your body. Love makes you feel light and exuberant. Repeat after me I can change only myself and no one else! I let go of regret and look to the present for joy. My love for myself exudes out of me and gives me peace.

A really good way to examine where you have been and where you are going with your behavior is to make a list of all the things you tried to change in your last relationship. Write it all down in a notebook. Now turn the page and write down what you actually did change by yourself. Thirdly make a list of where you want to go now. Examine the second list of things you were capable of changing. These are the things that are in your control and have to do with yourself. Stop worrying about someone elses behavior and life choices. You can not change someone else.

This was a big lesson for me to learn. I continued to bang my head against the proverbial wall trying though. He would not change no matter how hard I tried to make him. Until I stepped back away from the chaos and realized what I could do. Also I realized what I could not do.

My focus shifted to myself, what do I like about myself and what needs to change. I stopped being the victim and only concerned myself with what was in my own control. Miraculously my behavior changed, stress began to leave my body and a sense of peace came over me. It is truly freeing to realize that you have control of your destiny. You really had it all along, you chose to give the power to someone else. Never ever do that again. Only you can make the choices in your life that need to make you truly happy.

It can be scary to create the change in your life that needs to happen. Slowly face your fears and with each day you will grow stronger. Make an effort to accomplish a small thing everyday and celebrate it. Before you know it your life will start to feel right again. Tragedy is a part of everyone's life at one time or another. Learning important life lessons from it is valuable.

Thank You God For Today
A self-help book on domestic abuse

    Knowing the inner strength that you possess now should make you feel confident. Looking back on how far I had come. It was hard for me to believe that I once lived that miserable life that I saw looking back. I never beat myself up for it though and you should not either. Do not dwell on past problems only reflect and learn from them. Get better everyday and grow. Never be bitter about the dark days that were your past, for you have learned a valuable life lesson from this experience. Just always remember and never go down that dark, lonely path again. I have grown beyond ever being a victim and being controlled again. Through great sorrow comes wisdom.

Marybeth Rombach Nelson
Chapter 9,
Thank You God For Today

"One morning I woke up and there was peace." Oh how wonderful to have quiet and serenity in my home. The thought came to me how grateful I am for my new life that I have created. Thank you God for Today! I wanted to yell it from the highest mountain top so everyone could feel the joy that was back in my heart! No more drama to deal with. The day was mine to enjoy and to enjoy my children. I felt like a child again, anything is possible for my life. I am free from the controlling phone call and all of the manipulation. My life is a blank slate, to do whatever I wanted with.

Thank You God For Today
A self-help book on domestic abuse

If I can do it so can you! Be strong, choose the life that you want to have and go for it! Say positive affirmations daily to yourself. "I am a strong intelligent woman and there is nothing that I can't do if I set my mind to it." This is one of my favorite affirmations to lift my spirits and empowering too. Write down a positive affirmation and say it to yourself daily.

Focus on your goals to receive clarity for where you want your life to be. Envision the future you want to live. Find a room or place in your house that brings you peace and comfort. Sit in this room and write down your hopes and dreams.

Learn to meditate it can be a great stress reliever. Have only positive thoughts come into your head. Write down something daily that you are happy about. Have a list that you can add to that you are thanking God for daily. It always helped me to start the day off with a positive thought. No matter how bad things can be there is always something that you can be grateful for.

Ask God or your higher power to give you answers in your inner voice. Listen to your inner voice and acknowledge it. Write down your dreams and thoughts that are a sense of knowing where your life should be. Pray for guidance and clarity and you will receive it. Empower yourself with whatever makes you feel joyful. Life is supposed to be fun. Sometimes as adults we forget to let loose and just have fun. Your children will love it if you are goofy and joyful some of the time.

Appreciate your loving friends, enjoy them and stay in touch with them. If you are in good health acknowledge it. If you are lucky enough to have had a good education, be thankful. If you had great parents growing up, thank God for them.

Growing up my mother was always fun to be around. Her name was Virginia, she had a joy for life and the little things in life made her happy. My father Joseph also was very positive, even when he had tubes in his lungs after surgery, someone asked him how he was and he said great; how are you? Even though he was in a great amount of pain he choose to still be positive. I learned a lot from this great positive attitude and it makes you realize that any problem in life can be overcome.

Unconditional love is such a great love to experience. It gave me a foundation of knowing how great love can be. I wanted the great love my parents had. Both of my parents have passed but that unconditional love transcends space and time. I still feel it wrapped around me in every fiber of my being. I now know that I only need to love myself. If someone comes into my life that wants to respect and love me unconditionally. I am ready to accept it and reciprocate such love. Knowing that you can't force that kind of love or fix someone else has made me grow exponentially as a person. I used to feel sorry for people who did not feel loved growing up with their parents. But now I know they can learn to love themselves. You can't do it for them.

As your thoughts and actions begin to change so to will your life. Positive energy draws positive and keeps going. I believe in Karma and what goes around comes around. So let go of any anger, vengeance, bitterness and resentment. That person will get what they have put out eventually. You need not worry. Daily positive thoughts will help purify your life and give you focus.

Focus on what is good and continue to grow as a person. Take classes, read, join new groups, this will expand your knowledge and network of supportive friends in your life. The more positive people you have around you the better. It lifts your spirits, creates a great attitude and approach to every situation. Never ever forget that no matter how lousy the day has been there is something to be thankful for.

Keep faith in your heart that tomorrow will be a better day. The choice to be happy is yours and mine. Just adjust the attitude and make choices daily to make yourself happy. Open yourself up to the possibilities that you can achieve anything and everything that you believe is possible.

Positive self-talk will enable you to have the confidence to move toward your goals. Focus only on the good things in your life. Lighten up and enjoy the small things that make you happy, even if it is a piece of chocolate that you savor. Never doubt yourself, follow your instincts and listen to your inner voice.

Believe in yourself and others will too. Confidence can attract all good things to you. Build yourself up daily, with positive self-talk. Daily affirmations, help to focus a positive energy around your day. Tell yourself, "only good things come to me" I'm happy and whole in my life.

Empower yourself to success, with surrounding yourself with good people and friends. Pay attention to how you feel after you hang out with certain friends, only continue to spend time with people that build you up, not drag you down. Let hope come back into your heart and open up all channels of good things to come into your life today.

Do not doubt yourself, God made you special and your soul knows it! Trust that gut feeling, it is God's inner voice, your soul talking directly to you. Learn to listen and act upon it. The strength is within you, you just need to realize it.

Remove self limitations, realize what you are passionate about and go for it! When you have passion for what you are doing there truly are no limitations. Self-awareness is important right now to give you a clear picture of what you want in life. Slow down and try to learn how to meditate. It will help you clear your thoughts away and think clearly after you are done.

Write down short term goals and long term goals on a piece of paper or in your planner. Now realize that you can achieve these goals, no matter what your situation is. There are plenty of other people who have triumphed over tragedy. With perseverance and sheer will you can too. It is so exciting when the thoughts turn positive and positive action follows. Nothing is impossible! I love to read uplifting true stories about successful people who came from tragic beginnings. It truly shows you that belief and attitudes are the most important factors in achieving what you desire.

Perseverance, passion and free will are all it takes. Now empower yourself to achieve your souls purpose in this life. You will know it, feel it and believe it. You just need to discover it within you. It is there and I believe in you and know you can! Thank you God for Today, for the possibilities for my life are endless.

Marybeth Rombach Nelson

**Chapter 10,
Resources For Help in Getting Out of a
Dysfunctional Relationship**

No matter what your economic class or natural origin abuse crosses every culture and it is not your fault. There are many faces of domestic violence. Here are a list of resources to enable you to leave the abusive situation and protect yourself. Have a plan before you leave, where will you go? Do you have clothes packed in backpacks for yourself and the children? Do you have money set aside, not in the house that you can access? What agency are you going to call to help you? Have you filed a Personal Protection Order? Keep secret where you are going when you leave. Have a list of friends and family that you can go to for help. Select people that your abuser would not think to look for you at their house. If there is a friend or cousin out of town that you trust go there. Distance is a good thing, do not tell anyone else where you are.

Obtain a P.O Box for your mail to be sent to and always keep confidential your address, when filling out forms. This is so important and can help to keep you safe.

Do not use your address on a restraining order or police reports for obvious reasons. Use a P.O. box when ever filling out forms or a relatives address. Never list your address at your child's school publicly or in school contact list. Tell the phone company to have a unlisted number with no address publicly recorded. Also think about public forums, as facebook and online sites, never list the area you are in or where you work. Make sure settings are on social media are on private settings.

Never answer phone calls from unknown callers, block your phone number from showing up when you call people. Use generic message on your voice-mail. A paid phone card with a new phone number is a great way to go if you are leaving a abuser that you previously shared a plan with.

If you have children that are attending school, let them know what is going on. Have them copy a personal protection order if you have one. This is so important for the school to know not to release your child to anyone but you or who you have specified. Always carry a copy of your PPO with you at all times.

Change your routine if you are staying in the same area, go grocery shopping at a different store. If you are attending college let the campus police know you are being stalked and if you have a personal protection order give them a copy. Change where you park at college.

Do everything different to keep you safe, it may take extra effort, but it is worth it. When you leave, make sure you have time to get out safely. If he is going to work in the morning, make sure he won't return. Surprise him and leave when he won't be expecting you to leave. This will give you a whole day to get out.

The local police can be given the heads up that you are leaving, this way they can respond quickly if necessary. Call them ahead of time. Let them know you are getting away from a abusive person and want back up if they come home. Sometimes they will come to your house while you are packing up to ensure your safety. Also if you have not gotten a personal protective order yet, ask them for a fact sheet or information to help you.

It is known that the most dangerous time for a person being abused is when they leave the situation and the abuser. The abuser feels like they are losing control of you. So the situation is so very serious. Take every precaution necessary! Let your Dr. know what is going on and any other authority that can help you.

Make sure to have all your important papers, like passports, birth certificates, credit cards, titles to your car, bank account records and any documentation of your abuse. If you have bruising on your body take pictures and go to a Dr. to document them.

Thank You God For Today
A self-help book on domestic abuse

Press charges with the police and seek out domestic violence agency for help. Research stalking laws in your state and look up personal protection order at the local court house.

Michigan Personal Protection information http://courts.Michigan.gov/scao/selfhelp/protection/ppo_help.htm.

A personal protection order is in effect as soon as the judge signs it. You need to have the respondent served with the order usually through the police. Check your state laws.

In Michigan if a personal protection order is violated the respondent who broke the judges order is found guilty they can spend up to 93 days in jail or fined up to $500.00. The order is good anywhere in Michigan and can be enforced if violations occur. If a violation occurs and they are not arrested, you can file a motion to show cause, form cc 382. A "ex parte" order can be filed at no charge. The county clerk will know how to help you fill out the appropriate forms needed.

Once a order is signed the county clerk will give a copy to the police, whom enter it into Law Enforcement Information Network (LEIN). Always carry the certified copy with you. This is your proof that a order is in effect and to keep the abuser away from you.

The first thing you need to do is fill out the petition form at the county clerk of the circuit court. They have a packet put together for you called a personal protection order packet. Check the "ex parte" box if you are in immediate danger from your abuser. This is entered without a hearing and without prior notice to the other person or respondent. This is free to file, it does cost a fee to serve the respondent or abuser with a copy.

Make sure you read all of the instructions before you fill it out. Check off what you want the order to cover, 1. A petition requested respondent be prohibited from entry onto the premises, and either the parties are married, petitioner has property interest in the premises, or respondent does not have a property interest in the premises. 2. Petitioner requested ex parte order, which should be entered without notice because irreparable injury, loss or damage will result from the delay required to give notice or notice itself will precipitate adverse action before the order can be issued. 3. Respondent poses a credible threat to the physical safety of the petitioner and /or a child of the petitioner.   4. The respondent is the spouse or former spouse of the petitioner , had a child in common with the petitioner or is residing or had resided in the same household as the petitioner, has or had a dating relationship with the petitioner.   5. List the person's name_____ is prohibited from: entering onto property at, assaulting, attacking, beating, molesting or wounding your name_____. It talks about legal custody and parenting time orders provided removal of the children does not violate other condition of this order.

Thank You God For Today
A self-help book on domestic abuse

Stalking as defined under MCL 750.411h and MCL 750.411i that include but are not limited to: Following petitioner or appearing within his/her sight. Sending mail or other communications to petitioner. Approaching or confronting petitioner in a public place or on private property. Entering onto or remaining on property owned, leased or occupied by petitioner. Placing an object on or delivering an object to.

Property owned or leased, or occupied by petitioner. Interfering with petitioner's efforts to remove his/her children/personal property from premises solely owned/leased by respondent. Threatening to kill or physically injure your name_____.

Interfering with petitioner at his/her place of employment or education or engaging in conduct that impairs his/her employment or educational relationship or environment. Having access to information in records concerning a minor child of petitioner and respondent that will reveal petitioner's address, telephone number or employment address or that will reveal the child's address or telephone number. Purchasing or possessing a firearm. 6. As a result of this order, federal and /or state law may prohibit you from possessing or purchasing ammunition or a firearm. 7. Violation of this order subjects respondent to immediate arrest and to the civil and criminal contempt powers of the court. If found guilty, respondent shall be imprisoned for not more than 93 days and may be fined not more than $500.00. This order is effective when signed, enforceable immediately, and remains in effect until_____. 8. This order is enforceable anywhere in this state by any law enforcement agency when signed by a judge, and upon service, may also be enforced by another state, an Indian tribe, or a territory of the United states.

If respondent violates this order in a jurisdiction other than this state, respondent is subject to enforcement and penalties of the state, Indian tribe, or United States territory under whose jurisdiction the violation occurred.

9. The court clerk shall file this order with Michigan Sate Police/DPD who will enter it into the LEIN. 10. Respondent may file a motion to modify or terminate this order. For ex parte orders, the motion must be filed within 14 days after being served with or receiving actual notice of the order.

Forms and instructions are available from the clerk of court. 11. A motion to extend the order must be filed 3 days before the expiration date in item 8 or else a new petition must be filed.

_____

_____

Date and time issued
Judge

Thank You God For Today
A self-help book on domestic abuse

As you can see, this is a sample of the items covered on a personal protection order. It is one thing that you can file that will document all violations and put the abuser in jail if they violate the order. Obviously this is a piece of paper that can't stop a obsessed abusive person from harming you, so still take all precautions necessary to stay safe. You may also consider applying for a carry permit for a firearm. Take classes for self defense to also protect yourself. Be aware of your surroundings at all times.

Install dead locks on your doors, put in a security system on your home. Trim trees so you see outside. Put blinds on windows or drapes you can not see through. Keep your cell phones charged at all times. Sleep with a phone near you at night. Have a back up phone that is always charged. Keep outdoor lights on at all times. Consider adopting a dog for protection.

If you have children tell them not to answer the phone or door. Let them know to call 911 or have local police on speed dial. Don't scare them but make them aware of the abuse in age appropriate language. Tell them what to do in case of an emergency. Also self defense classes are also available for children.

Take children to a counselor and get counseling for yourself too. Many sexual assault agencies offer counseling at no cost or low cost for families. Also there are resources these agencies can refer you to. Make your children understand abuse and violence are wrong. Get away from anyone being violent or abusive and report it immediately.

A National Domestic Violence Hotline is
1-800-799-SAFE(7233)

Legal definition of domestic violence in Michigan is: MCLA 750.411h(a)-(e)

This section defines domestic violence for the purposes of getting a personal protection order.

Domestic violence occurs when a family member, household member, someone you have a child in common with, or someone you have dated or are dating:

← *Assaults, sexually assaults, attacks, beats, molests, or wounds you*

← *Threatens to kill or physically harm you*

← *Stalks you*

← *Interferes with your freedom, such as physically keeping you from leaving your home or kidnapping you*

← *Puts in you fear of physical harm, through words or actions.*

See Section 2950 of MI statutes page.

← Stalking is repeated or continuing harassment (at least 2 or more separate acts) that reasonably causes you to feel terrorized, frightened, "Unconsented contact" means any contact with you that is initiated or continued without your consent or after you have already asked that the contact stop. Unconsented contact includes, but is not limited to, any of the following.

- Following you or appearing within your sight;
- Approaching or confronting you in a public place or on private property;

Stalking

- *Appearing at your workplace or home;*
- *Entering onto, remaining on, or putting an object on property that you own, lease, rent, or that you are currently occupying;*
- *Contacting you by telephone; or*
- *Sending you mail, email or text messages.*

2, Aggravated stalking. Aggravated stalking means that someone is stalking you as defined above and on of the following occurs;

- At least 1 of the actions of the stalker is in violation of a restraining order of injunction and the individual has received actual notice of that restraining order;
- At least 1 of the actions is in violation of a condition of probation, parole, pretrial release, or release on bond pending appeal;
- As part of a the stalking behavior, s/he makes at least 1 or more credible (believable) threats against you, a member of your family, or someone living in your household;
- The stalker has been convicted of stalking or aggravated stalking in the past.

3 Posting or attempting to post messages about you. This occurs when a person posts sends, distributes, etc. or attempts to post a message about you through the Internet, computer or any other form of electronic communication without your consent, whether the information is true or not true. To qualify for a protection order under this ground, all

One of the following must be true:

← *The stalker knows or should know that posting the message could cause 2 or more act of unconsented contact with you (by anyone). See above for the definition of "unconsented contact";*

← *Posting the message is intended to cause conduct (behavior, acts) that would make you feel terrorized, frightened, intimidated, threatened, harass, or molested; and*

← *The conduct that comes from posting the message reasonably causes you to suffer emotional distress and to feel terrorize, frightened, intimidated, threatened, harassed, or molested.*

These are MCLA 600.2950 (1) a-j

This is how a domestic relationship PPO can help you. In a domestic relationship personal protection order, a judge may order the abuser to:

← *Stop assaulting, sexually assaulting, attacking, beating, molesting or wounding you;*

← *Stop threatening to kill or physically injure you;*

Thank You God For Today
A self-help book on domestic abuse

←

← *Stop stalking you;*

← *Stop contacting you or harassing you at your work place, residence, school, daycare (you must specifically request these places);*

← *Surrender any and all firearms and firearm identification cards to the police.*

←

←

← If there are guns involved in your case, the National Center on Full Faith and Credit (1-800-903-0111) may be able to help you find a lawyer to help you with your case.

A domestic relationship PPO may also:

← *Grant you temporary custody of your child;*

← *Prevent the abuser from interfering with your efforts to remove your children or personal property from the abusers home or apartment;*

← Protect or "impound", your address if you moved to escape abuse, so the abuser does not find out where you are;

← *Other reasonable requests that the judge believes are necessary in order for you to be free from the violence.*

Whether a judge orders any or all of the above depends on the facts of your case.

Marybeth Rombach Nelson

*State Domestic Violence Coalitions,
http://www.ovw.usdoj.gov/statedomestic.htm . United States Department of Justice*

ALABAMA <u>Alabama Coalition Against Domestic Violence</u>
*Post Office Box 4762
450 North Hull St
Montgomery AL 36103
Work Phone - 334-832-4842
Fax Number - 334-832-4803*

http://www.hotpeachpages.net/a/countries.html

Global list of abuse hotlines, shelters, refuges, crisis centers and woman's organizations, plus domestic violence information in over <u>80 languages</u>.

International Directory for Domestic Abuse resources

National

Domestic violence

One in four women (25%) has experienced domestic violence in her lifetime.

Thank You God For Today
A self-help book on domestic abuse

ALASKA <u>Alaska Network on Domestic Violence and Sexual Assault</u>
130 Seward Street, Suite 209
Juneau AK 99801
Work Phone - 907-586-3650
Fax Number - 907-463-4493

ARIZONA <u>Arizona Coalition Against Domestic Violence</u>
301 E. Bethany Home Road Suite C194
Phoenix AZ 85012
Work Phone - 602-279-2900
Fax Number - 602-279-2980

ARKANSAS <u>Arkansas Coalition Against Domestic Violence</u>

Victory Building
1401 W. Capital Avenue, Suite 170
Little Rock AR 72201
Work Phone - 501-907-5612
Fax Number - 501-907-5618

CALIFORNIA <u>California Alliance Against Domestic Violence</u>
PO Box 1798
1107 9th Street Suite 910
Sacramento CA 95814
Work Phone - 916-444-7163
Fax Number - 916-444-7165

Marybeth Rombach Nelson

COLORADO *Colorado Coalition Against Domestic Violence*
1120 Lincoln Street Suite 900
Denver CO 80203
Work Phone - 303-831-9632
Fax Number - 303-832-7067

CONNECTICUT *Connecticut Coalition Against Domestic Violence*
90 Pitkin Street
E. Hartford CT 06108
Work Phone - 860-282-7899
Fax Number - 860-282-7892

DELAWARE *Delaware Coalition Against Domestic Violence*
100 W. 10th Street Suite 703
Wilmington DE 19801
Work Phone - 302-658-2958
Fax Number - 302-658-5049

DISTRICT OF COLUMBIA *District of Columbia Coalition Against Domestic Violence*
5 Thomas Circle, NW
Washington DC 20005
Work Phone - 202-299-1181
Fax Number - 202-299-1193

FLORIDA *Florida Coalition Against Domestic Violence*
425 Office Plaza Drive
Tallahassee FL 32301
Work Phone - 850-425-2749
Fax Number - 850-425-3091

Thank You God For Today
A self-help book on domestic abuse

GEORGIA *Georgia Coalition Against Domestic Violence*
114 New St. Suite B
Decatur GA 30030
Work Phone - 404-209-0280
Fax Number - 404-766-3800

GUAM *Guam Coalition Against Sexual Assault and Family Violence*
PO Box 1093
Hagatna GU 96932
Work Phone - 671-479-2277

HAWAII *Hawaii State Coalition Against Domestic Violence*
716 Umi Street Suite 210
Honolulu HI 96819-2337
Work Phone - 808-832-9316
Fax Number - 808-841-6028

IDAHO *Idaho Coalition Against Sexual and Domestic Violence*
300 E. Mallard Drive Suite 130
Boise ID 83706
Work Phone - 208-384-0419
Fax Number - 208-331-0687

LLINOIS *Illinois Coalition Against Domestic Violence*
801 S. 11th Street
Springfield IL 62703
Work Phone - 217-789-2830
Fax Number - 217-789-1939

Marybeth Rombach Nelson

INDIANA *Indiana Coalition Against Domestic Violence*
1915 W. 18th Street Suite B
Indianapolis IN 46202
Work Phone - 317-917-3685

IOWA *Iowa Coalition Against Domestic Violence*
515 28th St
2603 Bell Avenue Suite 104
Des Moines IA 50312
Work Phone - 515-244-8028
Fax Number - 515-244-7417

KANSAS *Kansas Coalition Against Sexual and Domestic Violence*
634 SW Harrison St
Topeka KS 66603
Work Phone - 785-232-9784
Fax Number - 785-266-1874

KENTUCKY *Kentucky Domestic Violence Association*
PO Box 356
111 Darby Shire Circle
Frankfort KY 40601
Work Phone - 502-209-5382
Fax Number - 502-226-5382

Thank You God For Today
A self-help book on domestic abuse

LOUISIANA Louisiana Coalition Against Domestic Violence
PO Box 77308
1763 Physicians Park Drive Suite 1
Baton Rouge LA 70816
Work Phone - 225-752-1296
Fax Number - 225-751-8927

MAINE Maine Coalition to End Domestic Violence
104 Sewall St
Augusta ME 04330
Work Phone - 207-430-8334
Fax Number - 207-430-8348

MARYLAND Maryland Network Against Domestic Violence
6911 Laurel Bowie Road Suite 309
Bowie MD 20715
Work Phone - 301-352-4574
Fax Number - 301-809-0422

MASSACHUSETTS Jane Doe, Inc. - Massachusetts Coalition Against Sexual Assault and Domestic Violence
14 Beacon Street Suite 507
Boston MA 02108

MICHIGAN Michigan Coalition Against Domestic and Sexual Violence
3893 Okemos Road Suite B2
Okemos MI 48864
Work Phone - 517-347-7000
Fax Number - 517-347-1377

Marybeth Rombach Nelson

MINNESOTA *Minnesota Coalition for Battered Women*
60 East Plato Blvd Suite 130
St. Paul MN 55107
Work Phone - 651-646-6177
Fax Number - 651-646-1527

MISSISSIPPI *Mississippi Coalition Against Domestic Violence*
PO Box 4703 5425 Executive Place Suite A
Jackson MS 39206
Work Phone - 601-981-9196
Fax Number - 601-981-2501

MISSOURI *Missouri Coalition Against Domestic and Sexual Violence*
217 Oscar Drive
Jefferson City MO 65101
Work Phone - 573-634-4161
Fax Number - 573-636-3728

MONTANA *Montana Coalition Against Domestic and Sexual Violence*
PO Box 818 32 South Ewing Suite 108
Helena MT 59604
Work Phone - 406-443-7794
Fax Number - 406-443-7818

Thank You God For Today
A self-help book on domestic abuse

NEBRASKA *Nebraska Domestic Violence and Sexual Assault Coalition*
1000 "O" Street Suite 102
Lincoln NE 68508
Work Phone - 402-476-6256
Fax Number - 402-476-6806

NEVADA *Nevada Network Against Domestic Violence*
220 S. Rock Blvd Suite #7
Reno NV 89502
Work Phone - 775-828-1115
Fax Number - 775-828-9911

NEW HAMPSHIRE *New Hampshire Coalition Against Domestic and Sexual Violence*
PO Box 353
4 South State St
Concord NH 03301
Work Phone - 603-224-8893
Fax Number - 603-228-6096

NEW JERSEY *New Jersey Coalition for Battered Women*
1670 Whitehorse-Hamilton Sq. Rd.
Trenton NJ 08690-3541
Work Phone - 609-584-8107
Fax Number - 609-584-9750

NEW MEXICO *New Mexico Coalition Against Domestic Violence*
201 Coal Ave, SW
Albuquerque NM 87102
Fax Number - 505-246-9434

NEW YORK *New York State Coalition Against Domestic Violence*
350 New Scotland Avenue
Albany NY 12208
Work Phone - 518-482-5465

NORTH CAROLINA *North Carolina Coalition Against Domestic Violence*
123 West Main Street Suite 700
Durham NC 27701
Work Phone - 919-956-9124
Fax Number - 919-682-1449

NORTH DAKOTA *North Dakota Council on Abused Women's Services*
418 E. Rosser Avenue Suite 320
Bismark ND 58501
Work Phone - 701-255-6240
Fax Number - 701-255-1904

Thank You God For Today
A self-help book on domestic abuse

OHIO Ohio Domestic Violence Network
4807 Evanswood Drive Suite 201
Columbus OH 43229
Work Phone - 614-781-9651
Fax Number - 614-781-9652

OKLAHOMA Oklahoma Coalition Against Domestic Violence and Sexual Assault
3815 N. Santa Fe Avenue Suite 124
Oklahoma City OK 73118
Work Phone - 405-524-0700
Fax Number - 405-524-0711

OREGON Oregon Coalition Against Domestic and Sexual Violence
380 SE Capitol Spokane St Suite 100
Portland OR 97202
Work Phone - 503-230-1951
Fax Number - 503-230-1973

PENNSYLVANIA Pennsylvania Coalition Against Domestic Violence
6400 Flank Drive Suite 1300
Harrisburg PA 17112
Work Phone - 717-545-6400
Fax Number - 717-671-8149

Marybeth Rombach Nelson

PUERTO RICO Puerto Rico Coalition Against Domestic Violence and Sexual Assault
PO Box 193008
451 De Diego Street Rio Piedras
San Juan, PR 00926
Work Phone - 787-281-7579
Fax Number - 787-767-6843

RHODE ISLAND Rhode Island Coalition Against Domestic Violence
422 Post Road Suite 102
Warwick RI 02888
Work Phone - 401-467-9940
Fax Number - 401-467-9943

SOUTH CAROLINA South Carolina Coalition Against Domestic Violence and Sexual Assault
PO Box 7776
Columbia SC 29202
Work Phone - 803-256-2900
Fax Number - 803-256-1030

SOUTH DAKOTA South Dakota Coalition Against Domestic Violence and Sexual Assault
106 W Capital Ave #5
Pierre SD 57501
Work Phone - 605-945-0869
Fax Number - 605-945-0870

Thank You God For Today
A self-help book on domestic abuse

TENNESSEE *Tennessee Coalition Against Domestic and Sexual Violence*
2 International Plaza

Nashville TN 37217
Work Phone - 615-386-9406
Fax Number - 615-383-2967

TEXAS *Texas Council on Family Violence*
PO Box 161810
3423 Bee Cave Road
Austin TX 78716

Work Phone - 512-794-1133

Fax Number - 512-685-6240

UTAH *Utah Domestic Violence Council*
205 N 400 West
Salt Lake City UT 84103
Work Phone - 801-521-5544
Fax Number - 801-521-5548

Marybeth Rombach Nelson

VERMONT *Vermont Network Against Domestic Violence and Sexual Assault*
PO Box 405 5 School Avenue
Montpelier VT 05602
Work Phone - 802-223-1302
Fax Number - 802-223-6943

VIRGIN ISLANDS *Virgin Islands Domestic Violence and Sexual Assault Council*
Bay 20 The Village Mall PR #1 Box 10550
Kingshill VI 00850-9724

Work Phone - 340-719-0144
Fax Number - 340-719-5521

VIRGINIA *Virginia Sexual and Domestic Violence Action Alliance – Richmond Office*
5008 Monument Ave, Ste. A
Richmond VA 23230
Work Phone - 804-377-0335
Fax Number - 804-377-0339

WASHINGTON *Washington State Coalition Against Domestic Violence – Seattle Office*
1402 3rd Avenue Suite 406
Seattle WA 98101
Work Phone - 206-389-2515
Fax Number - 206-389-2520

Thank You God For Today
A self-help book on domestic abuse

WEST VIRGINIA *West Virginia Coalition Against Domestic Violence*
5004 Elk River Road
South Elkview WV 25071
Work Phone - 304-965-3552
Fax Number - 304-965-3572

WISCONSIN *Wisconsin Coalition Against Domestic Violence*
307 S. Paterson Street Suite 1
Madison WI 53703
Work Phone - 608-255-0539
Fax Number - 608-255-3560

WYOMING *Wyoming Coalition Against Domestic Violence and Sexual Assault*
PO Box 236
710 Garfield St Suite 218
Laramie WY 82073
Work Phone - 307-755-5481
Fax Number - 307-755-5482

If you, or someone you know, are a victim of domestic violence, sexual assault, stalking, or dating violence please know that help is available.

If you, or someone you know, are a victim of domestic violence, please call:

<u>National Domestic Violence Hotline</u>
1-800-799-SAFE (7233)
1-800-787-3224 (TTY)

If you, or someone you know, are a victim of sexual assault, please call:

<u>Rape, Abuse, and Incest National Network (RAINN)</u>
To be connected to the rape crisis center nearest to you, dial 1-800-656-HOPE (4673)

<u>National Sexual Violence Resource Center (NSVRC)</u>
1-877-739-3895

If you, or someone you know, are a victim of stalking, please call:

<u>National Center for Victims of Crime, Stalking Resource Center</u>
1-800-394-2255
1-800-211-7996 (TTY)

Thank You God For Today
A self-help book on domestic abuse

If you, or someone you know, are a victim of dating violence, please call:

<u>National Teen Dating Abuse Helpline</u>
1-866-331-9474
1-866-331-8453 TTY
You can also chat live on-line with a trained Peer Advocate from 4 pm. to 2 am.

(CST) daily.

American Bar Association Commission of Domestic Violence

www.abanet.org/domviol

The Commission on Domestic Violence works to increase access to justice for victims of domestic violence by mobilizing the legal profession.

American Domestic Violence Crisis Line

www.866uswomen.org

An international toll-free domestic violence crisis line that abused American women living overseas can call.

Asista *www.asistaonline.org*

Asista provides technical assistance in battered immigrant cases.

National Center for the A prosecution of Violence Against Women

www.ndaa-apri.org/apri/programs/vawa/vaw_home.html

National Clearinghouse on Abuse Later in Life

www.ncall.us

Southwest Center for Law and Policy

www.swclap.org

The Southwest Center for Law and Policy provides legal education, training and technical assistance on domestic violence, sexual assault, elder abuse, child abuse, abuse of persons with disabilities and stalking to tribal communities and to the agencies and professionals serving them.

Arkansas Coalition Against Domestic Violence

www.domesticpeace.org

Maine Coalition to End Domestic Violence

www.mcedv.org

Minnesota Center Against Violence and Abuse

www.mincava.umn.edu

New York Stat Coalition Against Domestic Violence

www.nccadv.org

Oklahoma Coalition Against Domestic violence and Sexual assault

www.ocadvsa.org

South Dakota Coalition Against Domestic Violence and Sexual Assault

www.southdakotacoalition.org

Wisconsin Coalition Against Domestic Violence

www.wcadv.org

Virginia Sexual and Domestic Violence Action Alliance

www.vsalliance.org

Take responsibility for your life today. I love this poem.

The Bottom Line, Author unknown
Face it!
Nobody owes you a living
What you achieve or fail to achieve in your lifetime
Is directly related to what you do
Or fail to do
No one chooses his parents or childhood
But you can choose you own direction
Everyone has problems and obstacles to overcome
But that too is relative to each individual
Nothing is carved in stone
You can change anything in your life
If you want to badly enough
Excuses are for losers
Those who take responsibility for their actions
Are the real winners in life
Winners meet Life's challenges head on
Knowing there are no guarantees
And give it all they've got

Marybeth Rombach Nelson

And never think it's too Late or too early to begin
Time plays no favorites
And will pass whether you act or not
Take control of your life
Dare to dream and take risks….
Compete
If you aren't willing to work for your goals
Don't expect others to
Believe in Yourself

I believe in you!

Thank You God For Today
A self-help book on domestic abuse

This poem is how I felt going through my time of turbulence.

>After Great pain, A Formal Feeling Comes
>By Emily Dickinson
>
>After great pain, a formal feeling comes--
>The Nerves sit ceremonious, like Tombs--
>The stiff Heart question was it He, that bore,
>Any Yesterday, or Centuries before?
>
>The feet, mechanical, go round--
>Of Ground, or Air, or Ought--
>A Wooden way
>Regardless grown,
>A Quartz contentment, like a stone--
>
>Tis is the Hour of Lead--
>Remembered, if outlived,
>As freezing persons recollect the Snow--
>First-Chill-then Stupor--then the letting go--

Once you take control back of your life and move forward, life will get better. Do not be afraid to let go and feel the sorrow. For in letting go you begin to heal your soul. Sometimes it seems like there will never be another tomorrow. Hope in the future is something to hold onto, for tomorrow anything is possible. Think of yourself and only how you can change you. You deserve to be happy and have a great life!

National *Domestic violence*

One in four women (25%) has experienced domestic violence in her lifetime.
(The Centers for Disease Control and Prevention and The National Institute of Justice, Extent, Nature, and Consequences of Intimate Partner Violence, July 2000. The Commonwealth Fund, Health Concerns Across a Woman's Lifespan: 1998 Survey of W omen's Health, 1999)

Estimates range from 960,000 incidents of violence against a current or former spouse, boyfriend, or girlfriend to 3 million women who are physically abused by their husband or boyfriend per year.
(U.S. Department of Justice, Violence by Intimates: Analysis of Data on Crimes by Current or Former Spouses, Boyfriends, and Girlfriends, March 1998. The Commonwealth Fund, Health Concerns Across a Woman's Lifespan: 1998 Survey of W omen's Health, 1999)

Thank You God For Today
A self-help book on domestic abuse

My hope is to touch your life and make you realize how special you are! The strength to leave is within you, life is too short not to be happy and healthy! So stop making excuses for why you must stay in a hellish relationship that is never going to get better. Focus on you, for you are precious in God's eyes and you can do whatever you set your mind to. Look at how you can improve your life and take action steps today.

There is no excuse for domestic violence, it is wrong the first time and every time! No other person has the right to abuse you in any way! The only one that can stop the abuse is you, by leaving. Stop doing the same thing and expecting a change in your circumstances. That change needs to come from you. There is a wealth of help out there waiting for you to reach out and ask for help. A better life waits for you, if only you will accept it.

http://www.dvrc-or.org/domestic/violence/resources/C61/

http://www.vachss.com/help_text/domestic_violence_intl.html

Marybeth Rombach Nelson

Wishing you peace in your
life today and everyday!
Contact me with your personal
story at: mb@thankyougodfortoday.org
 or marybethnelson@iknowcontentmbllc.com

Websites: Charity- WWW.HEARTWAVE.US
Book- WWW.THANKYOUGODFORTODAY.ORG
Business- WWW.IKNOWCONTENTMBLLC.COM

I would love to hear from you.
Sincerely from the heart,

Marybeth

Marybeth Rombach Nelson
Heart-WAVE, Women Against-Domestic Violence Empowerment
Email: createawave@heartwave.us

Empowering Women to take back their personal power
I Know Content MB LLC Publishing

Thank You God For Today
A self-help book on domestic abuse

One day, I want you to wake up and say Thank You God For Today and have peace in your life!

My next book coming out soon is titled,

On Angels Wings – Angelic Intervention

(A journey on how to become spiritually awakened)

Marybeth Rombach Nelson

About the Author:

Let me introduce myself, I am the author,

my name is

Marybeth Rombach Nelson,

Thank You God For Today is

a self-help book that comes

from the pain I experienced in

an abusive relationship.

One in 4 women experience

domestic abuse today.

Abuse is wrong the first time and

every time! There are many faces

of domestic violence and it crosses all

social–economic factors.

My hope is this book will help you to heal

yourself and to find hope for a better tomorrow.

Thank You God For Today
A self-help book on domestic abuse

God loves you and so do I

Sending you love and encouragement!

Made in the USA
Lexington, KY
12 May 2019